Emotional Intelligence

A comprehensive self help guide to developing EQ, managing anger, and improving your relationships!

Table of Contents

Introduction 1

Chapter 1: What Is Emotional Intelligence? 2

Chapter 2: Emotions Versus Thoughts 14

Chapter 3: Components of Emotional Intelligence 19

Chapter 4: EQ Versus IQ 36

Chapter 5: Strategies for Improving Emotional Intelligence ... 42

Chapter 6: Applying Emotional Intelligence in the Workplace 60

Chapter 7: Applying Emotional Intelligence in Personal Relationships 79

Chapter 8: How to Measure Your EQ 92

Chapter 9: Emotional Intelligence: The Dark Side 106

Conclusion 118

References 119

Introduction

Thank you for taking the time to read this book on emotional intelligence.

Emotional intelligence is the ability to recognize your emotions and those of others with the goal of understanding and managing these emotions. It is your ability to use emotional information to influence your behaviors as well as the behaviors of others.

Throughout the following chapters, you will learn how to measure your own emotional intelligence, as well as several ways to determine the emotional intelligence of those around you. Further, you'll be provided with a range of strategies to improve upon your emotional intelligence.

Emotional intelligence plays a huge role in our relationships. Not only those relationships that are romantic in nature, but also in the relationships we have with our colleagues, children, parents, friends, and others. A lack of emotional intelligence can lead to unnecessary misunderstandings, arguments, distrust, and even resentment.

Fortunately, emotional intelligence doesn't have to remain at a constant level. It can be improved upon continuously through many of the strategies provided in this book, allowing you to enhance your interpersonal experiences in all areas of life.

Once again, thanks for choosing this book, I hope you find it to be helpful!

Chapter 1: What Is Emotional Intelligence?

Have you ever felt so angry you couldn't think straight? Or you were so fired up by what someone said that you acted way too fast and then regretted your actions later? Well, guess what? You're not alone! Most of us seem to be tossed to and fro by our emotions. We leap before we look instead of the other way round.

Getting a firm grip on your emotions is vital if you want your life to be meaningful and happy. You have to be in the driver's seat of your emotions or else you will always act in ways that will cause you to experience regret. This is where emotional intelligence comes in.

As stated in the introduction, *emotional intelligence* is the ability to recognize your emotions and those of others with the goal of understanding and managing these emotions. It is your ability to use emotional information to influence your behaviors as well as the behaviors of others.

In simple everyday terms, someone who is emotionally intelligent:

- Is aware of their emotions.

- Uses the awareness of their emotions to deliberately control how they behave.

- Responds intelligently to others, thereby causing other people to be influenced by their behavior.

Emotional intelligence drives your behavior when you are at home with family and neighbors, at work with colleagues, or out socializing with friends. Every aspect of your life – your self-confidence, people skills, optimism, self-control, and even empathy – can be significantly improved by having a good understanding of your emotions and how to manage them.

Beyond having an understanding of the definition of emotional intelligence, it is important to know when to consciously manage your emotions. Generally, any situation that puts you under pressure – an emotionally charged situation – requires that you summon your emotional intelligence to help you wade through the waters of possible reactions that are available to you in such situations. Most of us usually don't allow our minds to see the options available to us, especially when we are in an emotional situation, because we have not trained our brains or consciously taken steps that will open up our minds to the options we have. So, we act first and then think later – a recipe for regret served with a topping of chilled embarrassment.

The way you respond to emotional situations determines your level of *emotional quotient* (EQ) just as your responses to situations that require rational and logical thinking determine your intelligence quotient (IQ). While it is true that your IQ can show how great (or not so great) your cognitive intelligence is, you need a high EQ to live a truly complete life. A person may score very high in their IQ testing but perform woefully on the EQ scale.

It is a lack of emotional intelligence which:

- Causes an otherwise bright and intelligent person to behave in such a way that leaves their personal lives in shambles.

- Makes a person acquire a great fortune yet remain unhappy.

- Causes an individual who is considered very powerful to become intolerant of others.

A lack of emotional intelligence is why poor managers always lose good people. People don't usually quit a job, per se – they quit working with managers who don't have good control over their emotional responses. Managers who are emotionally intelligent make it part of their unwritten job description to bring out the best in the people they lead or manage. The same goes for our homes, interpersonal relationships, and even in the way we perceive our individual selves. I describe emotional intelligence as an "unwritten job description" because emotional intelligence is not part of any official set of job duties, nor is it something you learn in an academic environment. However, it doesn't matter what your job is, nor does it matter how many people you manage; in fact, even if you stay all by yourself at home, you still need to learn how to manage *your* emotions and by extension, your behavior, for you to have any semblance of true success in your personal and professional life.

For you to live life to its fullest you must gain control of how you respond when you are:

- Under pressure to meet critical deadlines.

- Handling or dealing with an unruly child.

- Lacking in resources yet expected to perform optimally.

- Dealing with a difficult relationship (with coworkers or a loved one).

- Having an honest and open discussion with a significant other.

- Giving/receiving criticism.

In other words, emotional intelligence keeps you focused and rooted in the present moment so that you have a clear understanding of each of your interactions, both with yourself and with others. Emotional intelligence keeps you on track, making sure you do not go off on a tangent simply because you feel a certain way (usually irrationally) about a situation. You may feel it is most appropriate *"to give someone a piece of your mind"* because they behaved badly towards you. But the question is, would you still feel that way when you lay down to rest at night and really give your actions towards them a second thought? Here's the thing: you may never get the chance to apologize for your rash actions which is why you need to learn the exact steps on how to utilize emotional intelligence to make you behave in a way that is beneficial to you and to others.

Recognizing Emotional Intelligence in Everyday Life

So, how exactly do you know what emotional intelligence looks like in the real world? How do you know if you or someone has a high level of emotional intelligence? Here are some behaviors that demonstrate emotional intelligence in real-life.

Reflecting on Salient Questions

One of the foremost ways to recognize that you are becoming aware of your emotional responses to yourself, other people, events, and circumstances around you, is when you notice that you reflect on questions that would have, before now, meant nothing to you.

The questions could be something like:

1.   What could possibly be influencing this behavior from this person? Why is he or she saying this or acting this way? In effect, you are looking beyond the surface behavior so that your response to that person will be guided accordingly. For example, they may have recently received some very blunt negative feedback from their boss, and it is affecting their mood, so they are lashing out at everyone and everything in their path. Understanding where they are coming from may help you channel your response to them in a milder way.

2.   Are my thoughts at this moment a true reflection of what I truly want to say or do? Or am I being influenced by my current frame of mind? This line of self-questioning helps you to always check your words and actions against your already-established truths of what is right or wrong, so that you don't just react based on your moods, but based on your personal truths and values.

3.   Will this behavior display emotional strength or weakness? If I behave this way, will I be responding from a reactionary place or from a place of understanding? Essentially, what this question does is keep you clear-minded about the facts of a situation and how best to approach it.

When you start to ponder over these and other questions, it shows that you are beginning to exercise your emotional intelligence muscle. The more you engage in this type of behavior, the better your grip on your emotional responses.

Giving Thought to Your Thoughts

Our reactions are usually based on our perceptions. Things that happen are usually neutral; our *reaction* to the things that are happening, however, is purely from how we perceive those things – positively, causing positive emotions and reactions or negatively, leading to negative emotions and reactions. This means that when you get a good grip on your thought processes, it is easier to control your reaction or response to your emotions.

In other words, thinking about the thoughts you have when you observe something that is happening or what has happened will help you gain control over the emotions that are linked to those thoughts, and will eventually be aroused by those thoughts. This is a powerful display of emotional intelligence.

Pausing Before Responding

How many times have you committed to something or made a decision in the heat of the moment and then later regretted it? Making rash decisions is a clear sign that one lacks control over their behaviors. Taking control of your emotions will make you pause, no matter how briefly, and give a second thought before acting or speaking.

What I am driving at here is that emotional intelligence is called into action by a deliberate act of thinking about a response so as to avoid embarrassments. *"I'm sorry, I didn't mean to say that"* is usually an open show of a lack of emotional intelligence. It also signifies the start of a conscious realization of the tendency to act before thinking.

Later, when we discuss the strategies for improving emotional intelligence, we will take a look at a simple but effective exercise that can help you to take brief pauses before responding to whatever situation in which you find yourself.

Showing Empathy

Everyone seems to be right, at least from their own point of view. However, not everyone has developed the capacity to see things from another person's point of view. When you find yourself considering only your own perspective, you may be lacking emotional intelligence.

Putting yourself in the other person's shoes is one of the manifestations of emotional intelligence. You empathize with other people and feel what they feel. This helps you minimize labeling and judgment while deepening your connection with them.

Please don't get me wrong. Walking in someone else's shoe does not automatically translate into *agreeing* with them. No. What it means is that you are emotionally mature enough to temporarily put your personal views on hold so that you can try to understand their views and connect better with them.

Most of us do this when we go to see a movie. We know the movie is make-believe but we are willing to give up our perspective about reality and see the movie from the eyes of the actors. We do this so well that sometimes we cry when watching a sorrowful movie. At that moment, we have deeply connected with the essence of the movie and we understand perfectly what the characters are feeling. Also, we can thoroughly enjoy a comedy or action movie by temporarily setting aside our true perspective about reality.

When you apply the same principle to other people, then you are displaying a high level of emotional intelligence. The fact that you hold differing opinions from others should not stand in the way of your connection with them if you have a firm grip on your emotions.

Valuing Relationships Over Being Right

Transcending the ego is a difficult task for many but this is one way to show emotional intelligence. It takes one who is emotionally stable to say "*I am sorry*" even when they are clearly not at fault. They understand that apologizing doesn't necessarily mean that they are wrong; in fact, it often takes one who is more powerful to apologize to one who is weak. This doesn't mean tolerating everything that is thrown at you. It means that you adopt a quality of humility and have your eyes on more important things than being acknowledged as correct 100% of the time.

I am not suggesting you give up your rights. What I am proposing is that instead of bickering over who's right or wrong, those who have practiced being aware of their emotions would rather think carefully about an issue to see if giving up being right has any significant setbacks. If it doesn't, they simply let go. Emotional intelligence shows in your willingness to give up the dire need to be right all the time.

Do not confuse the need to be right with wishing to be proven correct in the long run. For example, if you accept going with the view of your significant other in the hope that sooner or later they will come crawling back to you in regret, you have simply put on an *outward* show of emotional intelligence and it has every tendency to backfire. If the situation doesn't go wrong (as you hoped it would), then you will start to build resentment towards them. And resentment is nothing but anger turned inwards – it makes you feel disappointed, frustrated, fearful, and mad each time you think about them and the particular situation that is causing the resentment. This is certainly not an attribute of someone who has mastered their emotions. A solid grasp of your emotions will show in your willingness to not only accept their view (for the sake of peace), but also have a genuine wish that things work out fine in the long run.

You Learn From Negative Feedback

As unpleasant as negative feedback can be, especially when there is no diplomacy in its delivery, an emotionally intelligent person will first of all muzzle whatever emotions that may prevent them from seeing beyond the rough surface of the negative feedback, and dig deep in order to learn a thing or two. Their focus is on how to improve with respect to the issue at hand, regardless of the method employed in giving the feedback.

Beyond learning from negative feedback, emotional intelligence will enable you to see clearly how the person giving the feedback actually thinks, especially if what they are saying is absolutely incorrect. So, instead of reacting negatively to negative feedback, an emotionally intelligent person will:

1. Either learn from it, or;

2. Understand the level of thought the other person has given to the issue they are talking about.

In both cases, you do not lose awareness of your emotions. Instead, you have used your emotions to your own advantage.

Giving Constructive Criticism

Ever heard of the "shit" sandwich? It is a way of delivering feedback that is not so pleasant without hurting the feelings of the person receiving it. This does not in any way water down the essence of the criticism, however, it presents it in such a way that the receiver knows that you are genuinely interested in their improvement. You are taking something as offensive as shit – the weaknesses of a person – and placing it between a loaf of bread – their strengths and positive aspects – to form a sandwich that the receiver will gladly accept. This is constructive criticism at its best, and it is a function of emotional intelligence. All you need to do is start with a compliment or remark about what they are good at or did well.

This is the first piece of bread. Next, you give the critical piece of feedback about what they could do better. This is the shit. Then, you finish it off with another compliment, the final piece of bread. This makes negative feedback much easier to take, and makes it a lot more likely that the receiver will take your feedback on board.

Inspiring People

It takes a special kind of practice to train yourself to focus more on the good in others than on their weaknesses. This practice can only become fully incorporated if you consistently resist the urge to get people to behave in ways that meet your own standards.

Emotional intelligence will make you shine the spotlight on their strengths by commending, praising, and showing appreciation for what they are doing right. People will be drawn to you because we all seek acknowledgment and will naturally gravitate towards someone who shares their appreciation for the things we do well. This, in turn, expands their strengths while diminishing their weaknesses as you help them channel their energies to become the best that they can be.

Forgiveness

Forgiveness ranks as one of the most difficult things for people to do. They cling on to emotional pains long after the deed has been done, making sure they keep the hurtful feelings fresh by reliving the events in their mind over and over again. This serves only one purpose: holding you back. You definitely cannot move past that point until you learn to forgive and let go.

Genuine forgiveness is a practical demonstration of emotional intelligence. It makes you realize that the only person staying put in a hurtful position is you. The other person who caused your feelings to get hurt may have moved on long ago, leaving you in a quagmire of bitterness and regret. A lack of emotional intelligence will keep you in that spot. On the other hand, emotional intelligence will set you free from the clutches of bitterness.

Are Your Emotions Working For You or Against You?

There are basically two ways your emotions work: either you let your emotions run wild and work against you, or you take charge of your emotions and make them work for you. The choice is absolutely yours.

Most people allow their emotions to work against them because they let their emotions operate by default – on autopilot. They get angry even when they don't want to, and they react harshly even when they'd prefer another form of behavior. It is as if they are the prisoners of their own emotions. Hopefully, you will, by the end of this book, learn how to take back the reins and be fully in charge of your emotions.

Keep in mind, however, that it is a gradual process. You cannot jump from being controlled by your emotions in one moment to being fully in charge of your responses to your feelings in the next moment. That type of quantum leap is not feasible and even if does happen, cannot be sustained.

Don't Be Sorry for How You Feel

It is not uncommon for people who are just beginning to learn about emotional intelligence to start to think that they are bad for feeling a certain way. Emotional intelligence is not about how you should or shouldn't feel, and it definitely isn't about thinking you are bad for feeling what you feel. South African poet, Ian S. Thomas put it beautifully when he said, *"Never apologize for how you feel. No one can control how they feel.*

The sun doesn't apologize for being the sun. The rain doesn't say sorry for falling. Feelings just are" (Thomas, 2012, n.p.).

The purpose of learning how to improve your emotional intelligence lies in gaining the ability to effectively control your responses to your emotions. It is never about stifling your feelings or emotions – these things are way beyond your conscious control. So, never feel bad for feeling bad! Instead, feel good for recognizing that you are currently feeling bad because that recognition is your key to thinking about your responses to the bad feelings you are having.

Chapter 2: Emotions Versus Thoughts

Do we feel before we think or do we think before we feel? Do our emotions produce our thoughts or it is our thoughts that generate our feelings? Or do they work both ways in an endless loop?

The debate about whether emotions lead to thoughts or thoughts lead to emotions has been going on for quite a while. However, I do not intend to make this book about that debate. I would prefer to show you the likely effects your emotions have on your thinking processes rather than engage in the debate of which one comes first. I believe that there is more to be gained by learning the practical application of these things rather than expending energy on debates. Whatever side of the fence you are on, I implore you to consider the following with an open mind. I do not intend to prove anyone right or wrong. I am simply explaining to you how you can use these insights to improve your own emotional intelligence.

Your Emotions Can Override Your Thoughts

Okay, now let's take a look at why you sometimes (or maybe even most times) act before you think even if you have a high IQ. What drama goes on inside of your brain when you find yourself acting before thinking? Why do you bypass the thinking brain under certain situations and jump into action before giving thought to your actions at a later time? Is there a "mechanism" inside of you that forces a temporal takeover of your rational mind during such situations? Let us attempt to answer these questions with a few simple but logical explanations.

I began the previous chapter by asking if you have ever felt so angry that you couldn't think straight or if you have ever been so swept away by what you heard that you acted fast and then regretted it later. I'm betting you or someone you know must have had these experiences or something similar to them. At those times when your actions didn't reflect those of someone who is rational, your emotions were in charge of your brain functions. Your emotions practically immobilized (temporarily) your ability to think straight. Regardless of your IQ score, when emotions run high they are capable of diminishing your cognitive ability, knocking you off from the seat of power so that you can't make good decisions, and then effectively thwarting your interpersonal skills. The outcome? You act before you think instead of the other way around.

Let me explain how all that happens in the simplest of terms. Don't worry; even though we will be talking about the brain, I assure you that there will be no medical or scientific jargon here.

Your brain can be classified into three major parts:

1. **The primitive (reptilian) part or brain stem**: This is at the root of your brain. It is designed to ensure that you stay safe, remain alive, and continue to reproduce. Think of this part of your brain as the survival part of the brain. Its primary function is to regulate your body by controlling your breathing, heart rate, sleep, digestion, and other organ functions. This part of the brain is pre-programmed and cannot be altered.

2. **The emotional (limbic) part**: This is the part that controls how you feel at any given moment. It has the ability to connect the information about your feelings to your memory. This part of the brain functions best when you encounter emotionally charged situations.

3. **The rational (neocortex) part**: This is the part of the brain that is in charge of higher level processes like reasoning, logic, language, and creative thinking. This is the part of the brain that is tested for IQ (McGill University, 2014).

Now, when you are in an emotionally charged situation (which, by the way, tends to be a common occurrence in our present society filled with too many emotionally upsetting triggers), an interesting drama takes place inside of your brain. Let us paint a little scene so that we get the message clearly.

The rational brain whistles along cheerfully, doing what it knows best – helping you to choose between options and intelligently communicating and interacting with your internal and external world. All of a sudden, a situation comes up that threatens your survival or reproductive functions. Immediately, your emotional brain jumps into a hyperactive mode and hijacks the functions of your rational brain. Instead of rationally thinking the situation through, the emotional brain, in one fell swoop, dislodges the rational mind, and then sends barrages of messages/signals and a swamp of impulses to the primitive brain like a quick succession of SOS messages. The primitive brain kicks into gear in a fight or flight response without giving the rational brain a second to think twice. All of this can happen in less than a second.

So, when you become really terrified like when there's a deadly snake in front of you, instead of waiting to fully assess the threat like a rational human would or should, the emotional brain temporarily shuts off your ability to think rationally, and you take off running for dear life. In this case, your emotional brain together with your primitive brain can save your life.

In another emotionally charged situation like when your boss berates you for something that is completely out of your control and not your fault, your emotional brain kicks into action, and you fly into a rage and give them a piece of your mind. In this case, your emotional brain together with your primitive brain could cost you your job.

As brilliant as our rational brain is, we still have the emotional brain and its over-guardedness to deal with. Because, until we do, our responses in words and actions under situations that are emotionally charged will stem from how we feel at that moment – our emotional state of mind.

Know Thyself

The phrase *"Know thyself"* has been around for quite a while. The implication, however, is not fully understood by many. Beyond knowing your name, your likes, and dislikes, "know thyself" means diving deep beyond the surface data associated with you to identify what actually makes you tick. To know yourself is not a one-time event. It is an exercise that should be carried out on a continuous basis because you are dynamic regardless of what your personality type might say. You may have taken a few personality tests – these days you can find a variety of them for free online. But does that automatically mean you have an in-depth awareness of who you truly are? To begin with, a lot of online personality tests are based on very old models, with some dating as far back as 100 years ago! That type of test cannot provide you with accurate information about who you are. You need more than an online test to actually "know thyself."

In order to have any significant control over your emotional responses, you must be able to:

1. Clearly identify exactly what it is that you feel and do.

2. Do exactly what it is that you want to do (eliminating or drastically reducing your automatic responses).

3. Do what you do for the exact reasons you choose.

The ability to function in this manner shows that you have a good knowledge of who you are and what makes you tick. You are not tossed around by your emotions, but rather you have a certain level of mastery over your behavior, especially when emotions are running wild.

But how can we possibly gain mastery over something as quick and as powerful as our emotions? Are emotions not completely out of our control? If the reactions in the brain happen so fast, what are the chances that we can stop these impulses before they ever occur? How do I succeed in my quest to know myself if these things are beyond my control?

Well, the bad news is that you cannot possibly stop your emotions just as you cannot possibly stop the chemicals in your brain from flowing. However, the good news is that you do actually have control over how you respond to your emotional impulses. It is true that these things happen very fast inside of your brain, but still, you do have enough time to avoid any rushed action if you take the time to "know thyself." This is the focus of the next chapter.

Chapter 3: Components of Emotional Intelligence

Reading between the lines you'll be able to see that there are some fundamental components, features, or abilities of emotional intelligence that we touched on briefly during our discussion in the first chapter of this book. These abilities can be improved upon by just about anyone who sets their mind to it. By the repeated and consistent practice of emotionally intelligent behaviors, you will essentially rewire your brain to behave differently under the same set of emotions that formerly tripped you up. What this chapter focuses on is how you can actually take your knowledge of emotional intelligence and put it to work in your favor, instead of against you.

Now let us break down emotional intelligence into its fundamental features so that we can learn their benefits and how to improve these abilities in our personal lives.

Self-Awareness

Have you ever paused to think what your innate strengths are - what you are naturally good at? Or maybe you have discovered along your life's journey that you are naturally weak in some areas. Perhaps you've observed that tasks that others cringe at get you all fired up and ready to give your best, or situations that others will shrug at and simply ignore can cause you to become enraged.

There's a sure way for you to discover your strengths and weaknesses: using the self-awareness tool. Your ability to accurately pinpoint your emotions, weaknesses, strengths, and subsequent actions are all part of what is known as self-awareness. It is the understanding of how your emotions affect you – your thoughts and actions. You see, the thing is, there's a slim chance of ever making any changes if you are not first aware that there is a need to change.

You are practically at the mercy of your emotions if you do not know that a lot of your behaviors are in direct response to the emotions you feel. This means, you have to take time to think about and become aware of your mood (how you feel, your emotions) and exactly what your thoughts about those feelings are.

So, the first step towards improving and strengthening your emotional quotient is to first become aware of who you truly are. Every other ability, skill, or feature of emotional intelligence is built on this very foundational one – the ability to become self-aware.

Self-awareness also means that you notice or identify your emotions and name them without being judgmental and reactive to the emotion. In other words, you must develop, bit by bit, the ability to become the passive observer of how you feel, especially in emotionally charged situations. For example, taking a brief pause to identify worry by saying things like, *"what I am feeling right now is worry over something that may or may not happen."*

Here's a brief description of what happens behind the scenes in your brain when you name your emotions without reacting to them. When you are in an emotionally charged situation, the part of your brain that is in charge of reactions in such situations (amygdala) becomes activated and will automatically drive you to take one of two actions: fight or flight. However, if you have practiced developing your self-awareness, the part of your brain that controls speech or language (neocortex) gets involved in the drama and prevents you from reacting to the emotion. Instead of reacting, your neocortex allows you to simply name or identify the emotion.

When you develop this ability to name your emotions without reacting to them or judging them as good or bad, then you attain what is known as metacognition – the knowledge and experience you have about your own cognitive processes. You stand aside and become aware of the happenings or experiences instead of being 100% wrapped up in the experience so much that you are barely aware of what is driving your response. By the way, metacognition is simply a fancy word for self-awareness.

Benefits of self-awareness

- A continuous understanding of yourself will help you in the choices you make.

- You live in the present. You are conscious of what is happening within and around you and can deliberately make choices to effect any necessary change you desire.

- You are true to yourself and your values. You don't have inner conflict because you are honest about who you are. You don't live a lie, and that is truly liberating.

- It is easy for you to handle negative feedback about yourself.

- You have a full understanding of why you behave the way you do. So, your behaviors don't come as a shock to you.

- You can improve your organization's output by working with people whom you have identified as being strong in areas where you know you are weak.

- Capitalizing on your strengths to reach your goals.

- Learning from mistakes instead of beating yourself up. Using mistakes as tools for growth.

- Helps you in taking calculated risks since you are fully aware of your weaknesses.

- You enforce healthy boundaries based on your strengths and weaknesses.

How to improve self-awareness

- Keep tabs on your emotions through journaling. Write down the particular trigger that caused a challenging emotion in you. The trigger could be a situation, a person, something that was said or done, and so on. Write down what you felt about the trigger, what you thought about your feelings, and how you behaved or responded. Equipped with this information, you are in a better position to understand your emotions, and then use that information to work on regulating yourself.

- Go through your day observing how others react to your behavior. If it is not possible to write down each observation, you can mentally note them and then see if there is a general trend. Is the general reaction from people towards behavior X negative or positive? What was the general reaction to behavior Y? This can help you look inwards and see if you need to correct behavior X or Y.

- You can ask for honest feedback from others – friends, family, and colleagues. If you are honest about improving your self-awareness, you will not be afraid to receive critical feedback from others. You will see it as an avenue to either improve an unhelpful behavior if you have any, or to understand how others think about you if their assessment of you was wrong.

Self-Regulation

Okay, so you have successfully identified an emotion that is welling up in you so fast it wants to just burst open and make you react in the most primitive of ways. But thankfully, you have quickly named it and slowed down the fight or flight process. So now what? What you are feeling is still there; it doesn't go away simply because you identified it.

The next step is to *manage* that emotion. Give it another outlet where it can effectively be channeled out so that it doesn't accumulate over time and result in an uncontrollable outburst.

Self-regulation or management is all about self-control. It is about how to effectively find a balance between restraining yourself from showing certain emotions and knowing when and how much emotion is appropriate for any given situation. Self-regulation is the ability that allows you to not permit emotions to get in the way of your tasks, goals, and purpose.

Please do not confuse managing or handling emotions with suppressing or numbing emotions. Your emotions are a natural result of your brain chemistry combined with your instinctive feelings – you simply cannot fight them off, nor should you try. Also, you cannot always control how you should feel at any given moment, but you *can* control your response to how you feel. That is to say, although how you feel may be out of your direct control, whether you react or refrain from reacting is completely under your control.

One other thing to keep in mind is that self-regulation or managing your emotions does not necessarily mean that you shut off all negative emotions and feel only the positive ones. That is impractical and attempting to live that way is basically trying to live a lie. The goal of self-regulation is not to numb your emotions selectively, but to consciously diffuse the effects of whatever challenging emotions you are having in any given moment. So, instead of attempting to stifle or squelch negative or challenging emotions, the focus is on embracing all your emotions and deciding exactly how and when to let them show or not show.

Here a few examples of self-regulatory behaviors:

1. An employer or boss who, instead of shouting and barking orders at his employees when he or she is stressed, delegates tasks and allows him- or-herself time to get their emotions under control.

2. A cashier who keeps their cool and remains polite even when a customer shouts insults at them for something that is not at all their fault.

3. A person who sticks to their healthy eating options in a quest to lose weight even in the midst of friends who are eating all sorts of "delicious junk."

4. A teenager who opts to study for an upcoming test instead of hanging out with their friends for an all-night party.

5. An employee who is denied their much-needed leave yet refrains from allowing that to make them go into a dark mood and eventually dampen their zeal for high performance.

6. An employee who refrains from yelling at their boss and damning the consequences when the boss is getting on their nerves.

Benefits of self-regulation

- It can reduce your chances of regretting your actions and utterances.

- When you really get the hang of self-regulation through consistent practice, you can become proactive about shaping your emotional tendencies.

- Your reactions stem from a rational place.

- You earn trust and respect from subordinates, employees, and colleagues.

- It makes you flexible and more adaptable to change.

How to improve self-regulation

- Always accept responsibility for your mistakes. Own them because that is the most effective way to correct them. Never shift the blame to others when you are guilty.

- Stay calm under pressure. Find a way to physically or mentally distance yourself from the situation that is causing the pressure. No matter how brief, each moment you spend away from the situation is a moment for you to self-regulate. Take deep breaths while you remove yourself from the situation.

- Accept change. Challenge yourself to see that change is constant, and the only way to not get hurt is to be willing to adapt to different changing situations without losing yourself in the process.

- Think about the consequences of your behavior. Before you act or speak, take a moment to consider what such responses led to in the past, what it is likely to result in now, and what the possible repercussions could be in the future.

Here are a few exercises that can help you improve your ability to self-regulate.

1. Practice mindful or controlled breathing exercises.

2. Reduce your stress levels by using self-hypnosis.

3. Get adequate sleep each night (7 to 8 hours of sleep is recommended).

4. Limit your intake of alcohol and increase your water intake.

5. Strike a balance between your work and personal life.

6. Create time each day for fun and hearty laughter.

7. Spend time alone where you can reflect on yourself.

8. Engage in regular physical exercise.

9. Engage in positive self-talk, affirming positive things to yourself.

10. Look at your behavior in retrospect to see if you could have behaved differently. For example, ask yourself: What was your behavior? How did other people react to that behavior?

Why did you behave in that way? Was there a better way you could have behaved given the same situation?

Self-Motivation

If you have ever watched someone who thoroughly enjoys what they do without giving thought as to whether or not they get money or status out of what they do, then you have likely seen someone who is self-motivated. Self-motivation is the ability to harness your emotions to help you achieve your goals, even when faced with seemingly insurmountable obstacles and challenges.

Self-motivated people are usually enthusiastic about their goals and are very persistent too. On the other hand, someone who lacks self-motivation – who cannot harness their emotions – can allow their emotions to run out of control and derail them from their goals. For example, under serious stress or pressure such as meeting a crucial deadline, if you are not self-motivated, the pressure to perform at your best within the shortest possible time (and perhaps under the most constraining of situations) can put you off. You can easily become angry, irritated, and give up on the task at hand. Conversely, being self-motivated can make you bring out your best to bear under intense pressure. You become more fixated on the task at hand to the exclusion of every other distraction.

Self-motivation leads to high performance. Instead of letting emotions drive you, you use the emotions to fuel your ingenuity. For example, instead of worrying and allowing that to mess up your mood and act irrationally out of fear that things might go wrong, you harness the feeling of worry and use that as your motivation not to fail at the task at hand.

Here's a more practical example. A clear example of a self-motivated line of thinking will go something like, *"It will be completely disastrous for my career if I don't meet this sales target this month. So I must put in my best, double my efforts, and think outside of the box."* A clear example of using your emotions against yourself will go something like, *"I'm doomed! There's no way I can meet this month's sales target. How am I ever going to survive in this job?"*

Self-motivation shows up as strong optimism – a firm belief that no matter what goes wrong, the individual will always find a way to achieve the goal at hand. An optimist will always think, *"I'm not going to allow the fear of failure to dissuade me from putting in my best."* This is the exact opposite of a pessimistic view about life. A pessimist will always think, *"It's no use to try. There's nothing anyone can do about it."*

Benefits of self-motivation

- The development of a firm belief in yourself and in your abilities. That is to say, it increases your self-confidence.

- Decreases the chances of procrastination and indecisiveness.

- It gives you a positive outlook about life in general. You become more open-minded and allow your creative juices to flow. It makes you a more fulfilled and happier person.

- It keeps your motivation high in spite of prevailing unfavorable circumstances.

- It builds your self-discipline.

- It helps you to maintain your vision on what you set out to achieve.

- It keeps you ahead of negative influences that can truncate your drive.

- It makes you confident to face the challenges that may appear in your life.

How to improve self-motivation

- Take time to discover your "why" – your purpose – for doing whatever it is you are doing.

- "*You've got to be hungry!*" That is to say, keep reminding yourself of this "why," because that will be the driving force behind your unrelenting efforts. Make it completely unthinkable to live without attaining your "why."

- Be prepared for setbacks. They will happen, but if you remain optimistic, then you give your mind room to come up with a way through, around, under, or over the setback.

- Look at the bright side. There is always something (at least one thing) positive about every setback, challenge, or roadblock along your path to accomplishing your goals.

- Break down your goals into smaller doable steps so you don't get too easily overwhelmed by lofty goals.

- Create momentum and maintain that momentum. Don't ever slow it down, even if you cannot increase the momentum further. For example, if you start out making 20 cold calls per day so that you can reach your monthly sales target, increase the number or maintain it. Don't ever go below 20.

- Keep a record of your performance. You can use this to measure your progress and know when to course-correct if you are not making significant progress in considerable time. Remember to reward yourself for even the slightest improvements.

- Take short breaks. Self-motivation doesn't mean a continuous grind. Don't beat yourself up for taking breaks, especially when you feel the need to. You are not being lazy; you are simply taking time off to recharge yourself.

- Do not be afraid of making mistakes. Mistakes show that you are making progress, you are making decisions, and you are not afraid of taking responsibility for what you believe in.

- Keep your motivation up by continually learning new skills. When you are stuck in repeating the same old pattern, you may get bored over time and get derailed. Tweak things, move things around, and apply new knowledge.

- Surround yourself with positive energy. Read books, watch movies, and listen to audio that keeps your motivation up. Associate with people who are also going for their vision and not backing down even in the face of tough challenges. You can also put up motivating reminders on your desktop background, on your phone wallpaper, and on the walls in your room or office space.

- Don't ever compare yourself to any other person. You do not know their "why," nor are you gunning for the same set of things.

- Give a helping hand to others who need motivation. You are not only helping them, but you are in turn keeping your own motivation up too.

Empathy or Social Awareness

When you hear the expression *"put yourself in my shoes,"* the other person is asking you to be empathetic to their cause. To be empathic means being able to identify, recognize, and understand the way other people feel. You have to develop the ability to recognize emotions in other people. Social awareness makes you become willing to temporarily suspend your point of view and see things from the perspective of another person. You are willing to understand what makes them behave the way they do, without judgment or prejudice.

For you to really be empathetic, you will have to see yourself in another person's situation or put yourself in their shoes. That means you will have to first connect with that emotion in your own self because if you do not know how that feels, you simply cannot fake the feeling. This is why self-awareness, the first of the fundamental features of emotional intelligence, is vital. You can only understand others to the extent that you understand yourself.

Being empathetic means that you are more sensitive to the feelings of others and you are able to read them clearly, even when they are not saying anything with their words. Non-verbal cues are not lost on you if you are empathetic to others. You are able to build better relationships with others because you are more sensitive, likable, and as a result, more outgoing.

Benefits of empathy

- It helps you to deliver feedback in a constructive way.

- It fosters team spirit in the workplace and at school, or in situations that require performing tasks cooperatively.

- Increases your compassion and understanding of other people's situations. For example, instead of growing annoyed that an employee has been recently coming late to work because they have an unwell dependent in the hospital, the empathetic employer or boss will be more open to working out something that will be a win-win for all involved, like altering their work hours or granting them a short period of leave.

- It strengthens your communication with others. You have an in-depth and genuine interest in others which automatically increases your connection with them.

How to improve empathy

- Practice listening to others without interrupting them or planning your response. Simply be present and listen to them to truly understand where they are coming from.

- Shift your focus from the differences between you and others to dwelling more on what you have in common with others. Allow your mind to come up with as many things that you share in common with the other person as possible.

- Broaden your horizon. Read more, learn more. The more you read and learn about diverse subjects and topics, the better you become at viewing things from other people's perspectives, and the more you become empathetic about other people's positions in life.

- Continuously engage yourself in critical analysis of your biases. Get in the habit of challenging your preconceived ideas or prejudices based on factors such as race, age, sex, and religious beliefs. Get in the habit of removing unnecessary barriers that can disconnect you from other people, so long as it doesn't make you lose your authentic self.

- Always give understanding a chance before jumping to conclusions or judgment.

- When interacting with people, practice gauging their feelings.

Social Skills / Relationship Management

This is the ability to manage and influence the emotions of others. Instead of compelling others to do what you want, you persuade them using their own point of view and motivate them to act without a sense of being cajoled or forced into action. You become a source of positive influence on others.

Positively influencing the emotions of other people means that you have been able to successfully manage your own emotions and also build empathy with others. This is the only way you can effectively influence positivity in others.

When you attain mastery of your relationships with others, you will be able to set the emotional tone for the interactions you have with others, tune into their emotions to see things from their angle, and then shift their perspective to sweep them into the realm of your own emotional state. What all this means is that you are bringing emotional benefits to the people you interact with. This will eventually result in a high level of likeness and trust in you as the bonds between you and others continue to grow stronger.

But this does mean that you should try to please everyone all of the time. Relationship management, or the mastery of your social skills doesn't mean dancing to the tune of everybody or pretending to be a certain way when you are not. It simply means being true to your personal values and truths no matter what, but keeping in mind the effect your values have on the people you interact with.

Benefits of social skills

- Helps to build a good rapport with others.

- Helps you widen your social circle and attract quality people to yourself.

- Improves your self-confidence and the ability to interact with all classes of people.

- It helps you in conflict management.

- Opens up doors of personal and professional opportunities for you.

- It makes you comfortable interacting with people you may not know. You can better communicate with large groups of people.

How to improve social skills

- Get in the habit of starting conversations with people even if you don't quite know them, and even when you are feeling nervous about it. The more you do this, the better you get at it, and the more comfortable you become at relating to strangers.

- Encourage others to talk during a conversation by asking open-ended questions, that is, questions that require more than a simple yes or no.

- Take a genuine interest in learning about other people's interests.

- Give honest, sincere, and generous compliments. It shows that you are friendly and makes others warm up to you.

- Let your words match your body language. Learn how to use your eyes and other body parts to connect to people without saying a word.

- Be polite to people, show gratitude, and practice general good manners.

Bottom Line

The fundamental components of emotional intelligence are interconnected. You need to improve in your use of each of these abilities in order to truly improve your overall emotional quotient. You may find that you are already good in some aspects, but deficient in others; you will have to work on your weaknesses so as to fully enjoy the complete range of benefits that are available to emotionally intelligent people.

Chapter 4: EQ Versus IQ

What readily comes to your mind when you hear the word "intelligence"? For many people, the word connotes high mental or cognitive ability, or something to do with knowledge and reasoning. While these are all great ways to see intelligence, they describe only one aspect of intelligence. Usually, when a mother says, *"My son is highly intelligent"* or when an employee says, *"I have a very intelligent boss,"* they are most likely referring to the ability of the person to utilize their power of fluid reasoning or some other ability that is related to just one form of intelligence, which is the IQ or intelligence quotient.

The questions that need some thoughtful consideration are:

- Does intelligence quotient alone guarantee that a person is highly successful?

- What other forms of intelligent traits are available to we humans?

- Can we become successful if we focus our attention on developing only one aspect of intelligence?

The fact that you may not be good at calculating the time it takes for light to travel from the sun to your open window doesn't not necessarily mean you cannot be smart in other areas, like being able to find someone to help fill the gaps where you are deficient, or to easily read other people like an open book.

Over the years, quite a number of psychologists have proffered different types of human intelligence to include: creative intelligence, practical intelligence, and analytical intelligence. There have been other theories that further categorize human intelligence to include: linguistic intelligence, existential intelligence, musical intelligence, naturalist intelligence, intrapersonal intelligence, interpersonal intelligence, and so on.

For the purposes of this book, we shall only be considering 3 broad forms of human intelligence, namely:

1. Intelligence quotient (IQ)
2. Emotional intelligence (EI) or Emotional quotient (EQ), and
3. Social intelligence

Intelligence Quotient (IQ)

People who have high natural abilities in areas like spatial processing, visual processing, quantitative reasoning, and fluid reasoning, among others, are said to have a high IQ. Their cognitive functions top the charts, and they are usually looked upon as people who are likely to be generally very successful in life.

IQ is derived from standardized tests designed to measure an individual's intelligence based on their cognitive abilities. It is usually a number arrived at by dividing the test taker's mental age by their actual age, and then multiplying the result by 100. For example, if your age is 20 and your test shows that your mental age is somewhere around 25, your IQ is 125, that is, 25 / 20 x 100. In more recent IQ tests the individual's result is arrived at by comparing their score to that of others in their age group.

Although having a high IQ is desirable because it puts you ahead of others in your age group as being capable of high performance with regards to cognitive abilities (especially in the areas of academics and business), a high IQ alone does not automatically mean you will be a happy and fulfilled person, even if you become very successful in your chosen career.

This is why you find a lot of high performers and achievers living unhappy lives. They have dedicated their focus to the pursuit of only one aspect of human intelligence to the neglect of other aspects. You may have met or heard of people who are "smart" yet they fail woefully when it comes to interpersonal and intrapersonal skills. It is not uncommon to see people who have come up with groundbreaking discoveries in science or in business, but they don't know a thing about building rapport with other people. They may possess a very high IQ, but on the EQ scale, they are very far behind.

For the human to live truly and happily, there must be an equal amount of importance placed on *all* aspects of human intelligence. In other words, you must be as 'street smart' as you are 'book smart' to live a truly successful life.

Emotional Quotient (EQ)

Emotional quotient is the measure of your emotional intelligence. EQ measures how well a person can:

- Identify their emotions

- Take control of their emotions

- Relate to others

- Perceive and evaluate the feelings of other people

- Use emotions to create rapport and boost social interaction

There are different types of tests that are designed to measure EQ. We will take a look at how to measure your EQ in a later chapter. However, keep in mind that no matter what the result of your EQ test currently is, there is always room for improvement.

While having a high IQ usually means you are ahead of the pack and can perform better especially in business and in academics, EQ is still required for you to become a great leader or even just a better colleague. Little wonder some organizations now require an EQ test during their hiring process.

The problem with a lot of people is that they know that they don't rank high on the IQ scale, so they presume they are not intelligent in any other way, since the IQ is the only type of intelligence measure that they are familiar with. *"I'm not good with numbers, nor am I good with linguistics. I'm just useless!"* But that is very far from the truth! What you need is to first begin to take the steps to become self-aware – learn what your strengths and weaknesses are. Then follow up with the other steps of improving your emotional intelligence.

Writing yourself off because you don't have the IQ of Einstein is being very unfair to yourself. Having a high IQ is good, but what is better is to have a high IQ plus a high EQ; that would be the true definition of a well-rounded genius!

IQ is very important, but that does not mean it is the only factor that results in success. And by the way, you can improve your IQ too; it is not carved in stone, although it tends to remain roughly the same throughout a person's life. But that is not the focus of this chapter. A lot of importance has been placed on IQ while neglecting other areas of human intelligence. This can only result in "half-baked" success. The purpose of this chapter is to highlight the necessity of developing the other aspects of intelligence that are equally as important as the IQ.

Social Intelligence

This type of intelligence is usually deeply intertwined with emotional intelligence; both share a lot of similarities. In fact, if you develop your emotional intelligence, you may have covered all you need to become socially intelligent, as well. Nevertheless, there is a slight difference between the two.

Although both of these are connected to the ability to navigate emotional and social situations, social intelligence focuses on the future, while emotional intelligence deals with handling emotions in the present.

Social intelligence is more concerned with how to understand the behaviors, feelings, and the possible different personalities within you and others, and how to apply this knowledge in order to arrive at positive outcomes in the future.

Bottom Line

As much as it is desirable to be book smart, there is an equal need to be a fully rounded human being, especially in the society we now live in. The notion that one form of intelligence is better than the other is not the message I am aiming to pass across. My intent here is very simple and clear: you must strive to find a balance in your quest for developing your intelligence. That is how to become a truly successful leader, boss, employer, employee, student, parent, child, friend, colleague, and team player. To pursue only one form of intelligence while neglecting the others is to live an unbalanced life. It may get you accolades, awards, and recognition, but it will leave you unhappy and unfulfilled.

To quote Daniel Goleman, author and science journalist who popularized the term emotional intelligence: *"If your emotional abilities aren't in hand, if you don't have self-awareness, if you are not able to manage your distressing emotions, if you can't have empathy and have effective relationships, then no matter how smart you are, you are not going to get very far."*

Chapter 5: Strategies for Improving Emotional Intelligence

Execution

Learning about emotional intelligence is all good and fine, but beyond all that knowledge is the next step of actually applying or executing what is learned. Your desire to improve your emotional intelligence is commendable, nevertheless, you must be willing to move from the place of acquiring the right knowledge and testing your EQ to the place of taking baby steps towards the actual implementation of emotional abilities in the real world.

There are a lot of challenging situations that you may face daily. Some of these challenging situations may include:

- Compassionately managing an employee when they have personal issues.

- Choosing between attending to your spouse or child when both require your urgent attention.

- Finding an equilibrium between accountability and empowerment with your teenager or a subordinate at work.

- Helping out a child who is feeling left out among their peers.

- Giving critical feedback to a colleague or employee.

- Managing a customer who is mad at you for no good reason.

- Deciding where to invest your money.

- Handling your child who is throwing a tantrum in a toy store because you didn't buy them their favorite toy.

- Figuring out which vendor to engage, given past disappointing experiences.

The list goes on. It almost seems as if we go from one challenging situation to another every single waking moment of our lives. This is why moving past mere "head knowledge" to developing the inner emotional strength to apply emotion management skills is important. Execution is the only way you can move from feeling stuck to a gradual feeling of improvement.

Here are 7 actionable steps you can begin to take right now to increase your capacity for executing your emotional abilities:

1. **Write down your triggers**: What may be a challenging emotional situation for one person may not be the same for you. There is no one particular situation that puts everyone into an emotional frenzy. Identify yours and write them down in a special emotional intelligence journal. Perhaps when your child cries and throws a tantrum "unnecessarily," that triggers in you the feeling of anger or frustration and affects how you react to the child or any other person who comes in contact with you at that moment. Write "child tantrum" in your journal as one of your triggers. Go through your day with the intention of identifying as many triggers as you can; not because you want to deal with these triggers there and then, but simply to identify them. Oh, and by the way, identifying your emotional triggers is actually activating and involving the language part of your brain during an emotionally challenging situation. And that, in

itself, is a step towards improving your emotional intelligence.

2. **Implement strategies for handling your triggers**: The next thing to do is to write down the strategies that are available for intelligently handling the identified triggers. Now, rehearse what you will do in those difficult emotional situations in your mind, or in front of a mirror if you like to make it more practical. The more time and effort you put into rehearsing, the better you will get at handling the real-life situations.

3. **Work on your general outlook about life**: Your outlook on life affects your mental-emotional frame of mind. If you are dominantly negative about life – being *pessimistic* – you need to begin to gradually shift your view to become *optimistic* about life. This doesn't happen overnight, so don't beat up on yourself if you still find yourself being cynical or negative from time to time. The important thing is for you to first recognize that you are in a place that does not give you a good chance of controlling your behavioral response. Once you have identified that fact, it makes it more likely that you will begin to work on shifting that perspective. So, a practical step in this direction is to begin to write in your journal five or more things you are grateful for each day. If that sounds too spiritual or too "new age" for your liking, consider writing down at least 5 good things about every challenging situation in which you find yourself.

4. **Set reminders**: With the hustling and bustling lifestyle almost all of us have come to accept as normal, it is often easy to disconnect from how we feel in each moment. This disconnection from your emotions is one of the culprits for behaving irrationally when something

unexpected happens out of the blue. To help you stay connected for the most part of your busy day, set reminders in the form of alarms or timers on your phone, laptop, or even your good old alarm clock if you use one. As the alarm goes off at different intervals during your day, take a brief moment to notice how you currently feel emotionally. Try to pinpoint the emotion currently coursing through your mind, and if it is something you need to change or work on, quickly tie that back to the first step of writing down what triggered the emotion.

5. **Think deeply about your opinions**: Your perspectives shape how you view the world. When things challenge your tightly held opinions, it can cause you to feel very negative about the source of that challenge, especially if you have not deliberately developed the ability to look at things from opposing perspectives. For you to accept the changes that will come from implementing emotional intelligence strategies, you need to be willing to think deeply about your opinions, especially the ones that are dear to you. You do not need to change every single opinion you hold, but being willing to take a look at an opposing viewpoint (even if you are not necessarily agreeing with it) is a great way to keep an open mind and be receptive to higher arguments, or new and better ideas.

6. **Give up the blame game**: You are 100% responsible for your emotional response. Your behavior comes from you, not from any other person. So, stop blaming someone or something outside of you for what you say or do in response to any situation. The moment you begin to accept full responsibility for your emotions and behaviors, you set yourself up for a life of course-correction and rapid growth.

7. **There is no graduation day**: There is no graduating from this school of emotional intelligence. It is a continuous learning process. Your goal should be to keep on improving by the day, not looking forward to the day that you will become some sort of "guru." Remember, if you are green (learning), that means you are growing, but the moment you become ripe (stop learning), you begin to get rotten (stop improving).

Okay, now that you know exactly the steps to take to increase your chances of applying emotional intelligence strategies in real life, let us turn our attention fully to learning the strategies themselves. Some of these strategies may appear too simple or too common to have an impact, but trust me, they have all been proven to be very effective at improving the way you respond to emotional challenges. I will suggest that you begin with just a few and get real used to them, and then continue to add more from the list as you see fit. It will be quite overwhelming to try and implement everything on this list at one go. In fact, doing so successfully would be close to impossible. Just take baby steps, and you will be sure to notice significant improvements within considerable time, as long as you remain consistent in your application.

Strategies

Take Brief Pauses Before Responding

Here's an exercise that has helped me improve my responses whenever I find myself in an emotionally charged situation. I will recommend you practice this over and over again to make it into a habit. When you are in a very emotional moment, take a brief pause and ask yourself these three questions before you say a single word or respond to the situation:

1. Is it absolutely necessary to say this or respond to this?

2. Is it absolutely necessary that I should say this or respond in this way?

3. Is it absolutely necessary that I should say this or respond in this way *now*?

This may seem quite simple and indeed it is, but it is certainly not very easy to implement. Do not be fooled by the simplicity of this little exercise; the effect of it over time can be quite fascinating.

Many people do not pause to ask themselves these questions, that is why you see a lot of misunderstandings in relationships, hostile comments on social media, people always apologizing for judging too quickly, and meetings that are unnecessarily long as people go back and forth saying and unsaying things they mean and don't mean.

Although this exercise may sound too easy in theory, it is very difficult to remember to ask these questions in real-life situations. The reason is simple: most people are not used to taking brief pauses before they react or respond to situations. Their emotions always have the better of them! It will take quite some practice and effort for this to become a useful habit, but the reward is worth the effort.

Just Stop

We live in a world that makes us feel that there is a need to respond and react to everything that is happening in and around us. We want to react to every remark, email, phone call, text message, rumor, body language, news, and so on.

Develop the habit of deliberately allowing yourself to simply watch things happen without the urgent desire to respond or react to them, at least not immediately. Your world will not come crashing down if you delay your response to things that are happening.

When you catch yourself in the act of trying to react urgently as if your life depends on your response, stop! Take a pause. Drink a glass of water. Do anything except react immediately. The act of stopping yourself will help you to think about your reaction before doing something you will later regret.

Practice Mindfulness

Living in the moment seems to be a very difficult task for many people. They are either worried about the future or are stuck thinking about a not-so-pleasant past. They are completely disconnected from the present moment. This is why, when something happens in the present moment that jars them back into the here and now, they tend to react before thinking about it rationally. Being present – inhabiting your moments – will keep you aware, and you can sense when someone or something is about to trigger a negative emotional response in you and then take appropriate steps to manage the situation.

There are several activities or exercises that fall into the category of mindfulness. The most common ones are meditation, conscious breathing, and tuning into your environment.

- **Meditation**: There are several types of meditation all aimed at achieving different goals. The type of meditation I would recommend is short periods of time in silent observation of your thoughts, emotions, and sensations with the goal of simply noticing the activities that go on in your mind. When done properly, meditation can effectively help you become more self-aware. So, take 5 to 10 minutes out of your daily schedule to simply observe the contents of your mental-emotional framework. With regards to enhancing your emotional intelligence, there is really no point in setting aside one special period of time, where you will sit in absolute silence with your legs crossed, back erect, and depriving yourself of all thoughts for an hour or even more. While that type of meditation may be suitable for other noble purposes, it is not a requirement for improving your emotional intelligence. I suggest you spread your meditation throughout your day at different intervals of short amounts of time. Even if you can't find 5 straight minutes, a few minutes of deliberate silent observation of your inner workings several times a day over a considerable period will do wonders for your overall emotional well-being.

Meditation has been scientifically proven to reduce depression, nervousness, anxiety, and general stress. It also helps to improve your metacognition ability, controls impulsive behaviors, improves your brain performance, as well as improving awareness of the self. With all these benefits, it would be such a waste of a powerful tool that is within everyone's reach if we do not practice mindfulness meditation.

- **Conscious breathing**: We all breathe. So, how does breathing affect our emotional state of being? By taking deep conscious breaths, you are giving your body and mind a signal to pause and disconnect (at least temporarily) from whatever is happening within and outside of us. Breathing consciously brings you back into the moment and makes you want to think about what you are feeling. When you feel a wave of emotions coming on, it is a good practice to just take a few seconds to breathe deeply. You can also count backwards from 10 to 1 while you are breathing slowly. Alternatively, you can inhale and hold the air in while you count up to 4 and then exhale and hold while you count up to 4 again. Repeating this breathing exercise 4 or 5 times can help you to regain control over whatever emotions you were feeling before you started the exercise.

- **Tuning into your environment**: As you go about your daily activities, deliberately become mindful of the things happening around you. When you meet someone, be present with them as you greet and smile at them with genuine gestures – a handshake, hug, kisses, or a simple wave. Take a moment to just observe people (family, friends, neighbors, colleagues, and even strangers) without any critical thoughts or judgments about them. See what they are currently doing and simply appreciate who they are and what they do. When you take a walk, don't tune out the entire world and fix your attention only on where you are headed. There are a plethora of things along your path; take the time to connect with these things, feel the wind on your skin, listen to the sounds around you, feel the sun's rays on your body, see the skies above you, observe the road you walk upon, notice the way your body moves, and so on. Of course, this practice should also be done for a short period of time. Spending your entire day in awe of your environment will amount to being unproductive – unless of course, you do not intend to be productive for that day. This practice helps you to stay connected to your external world and the people you interact with.

Get Some Body Movement

Sometimes all you need to change your emotions and mood is to do something that will dramatically change your physiology – your body movement. Go for a jog or a full run, jump around, do a workout, go and play with the kids at the playground, take a walk in the woods or in your neighborhood, change the position of things in your room or office – just do something that will snap you out of that negative mood, especially when you are feeling depressed, down, and blue.

Here's a simple trick that is sure to get your mind thinking differently when you are feeling powerless, anxious, or overwhelmed. Stand in a power pose; hands on your hips with your legs spread wide apart and your head raised high like a superhero! Make sure that your body occupies a lot of space, just as a confident person would. Hold that pose for few seconds and you will be amazed how your body chemistry will change from feeling down to feeling optimistic. The power pose sends a clear message to your brain: I can do this! And immediately your brain begins to release chemicals that will help you accomplish the current task at hand.

Watch What You Eat/Drink

What you eat has a lot more to do with your moods than you may realize. Self-regulation or self-management becomes a lot easier when you pay attention to the foods that go into your mouth. You may do all other things right as far as self-regulation is concerned, but if you ignore this aspect you may find that it trips you up at the most unexpected moment. Bottom line: eat well. Eat balanced meals. Stay away from eating junk food as much as possible. But beyond *what* you eat, consider also *when* you eat. So, inasmuch as you are careful about the quality of food you consume, keep your mind also on the rate and intervals at which you eat. Overstuffing yourself with food can have a massive negative effect on your emotions.

One reason people eat too much is by eating mindlessly. Yes, mindfulness also comes into play when eating, if what you consume is going to have a positive effect on your body. What are your habits when you eat? Are you focused on the food, or is your attention on the TV, your phone, or on some book? It is very common for people to grab the TV remote when eating. I strongly suggest that the only reason your hand should reach for the TV remote while you are eating is to turn off the TV!

It goes without saying that consuming too much of any intoxicants can hamper our ability to think rationally. You can't be drunk and expect to manage your emotions effectively. It is an error to think that alcohol and other intoxicants can keep emotions like depression and anger in check. If you assume, "*A shot of alcohol will make me forget all these stupid worries!"* Well, guess what: it drives you more into a depressed state and worsens your worries. I am not suggesting that you completely stop your alcohol consumption; this is an entirely personal decision only you can make. However, I am recommending that you significantly cut down your alcohol intake (if alcohol is your thing).

Get Interested

Whether it is a personal or professional matter, once you lose interest in the subject, you begin to get bored with it. And once boredom sets in, impatience is likely to follow. For example, once you lose interest in a line of discussion during a meeting, you may find yourself feeling like the meeting is dragging on and should have ended already! Whoever is bringing up new subjects to be discussed is simply fueling your impatience. It is not unlikely that you will find yourself getting irritated by harmless comments by others in the meeting. Your emotions are already getting the better of you. If it is a one-on-one discussion, perhaps with a salesperson who is trying to sell you with their well-practiced sales pitch, once you get disinterested, you may find yourself completing their sentences to subtly tell them, *"I already know this. Just get it over with!"*

One key factor in self-regulation – a fundamental component of emotional intelligence – is to keep yourself interested in the subject matter at hand. Question: How exactly do you keep yourself interested?

1. Practice active listening – think about the words the other person is saying.

2. Temporarily suspend your disbelief – just flow with what they are saying even if it is only for that moment. Amuse

yourself by seeing how far their opinions will go. After all, it is a sign of mental maturity to be able to hold two opposing opinions in your mind without losing control of your ability to function.

3. Enjoy a different perspective – what someone may be telling you could be far off from what you know is correct, but allow your mind to welcome a different, but not necessarily fresh, perspective from what you are used to.

4. Ask questions – give the other person an opportunity to explain exactly what they mean. This may open up a new learning avenue for you.

However, if you honestly don't have any interest in the subject, be assertive enough to speak up whether in a one-on-one situation or in a meeting. Be bold, but calm and unassuming. You can say something like, *"I get your point. Can you round this up please?"* Or, *"I'd love to hear your full presentation, but I'm running out of time. I'd really appreciate it if you could summarize this."* Here's an example you can use in a meeting. *"In my opinion, I think we have covered enough ground on this issue. If there is nothing new to add, I'd suggest we move on to something else or adjourn this meeting."* But if you are not in a position to make such remarks, you can simply excuse yourself from the meeting and clear your head outside for a while before returning.

Pay Attention to Your Intuition

It's difficult to develop a keen sense of self-awareness without also developing the ability to pay close attention to your intuition. This is especially necessary when you are unsure which decision to make or what path to tread. Intuition may seem a rather tricky tool to use (and somewhat abstract, I may add), but if you keep fine-tuning your listening skills, you will eventually get the hang of it. Those who are emotionally intelligent enough to hone on in their intuition can almost always predict with high accuracy when a situation will likely turn out bad. They appear prepared for the situation.

Set Goals

Self-motivation can hardly be maintained without having something to look forward to. If you are not giving yourself tasks to accomplish, you are not giving yourself enough motivation.

Goals give you direction for the long-term and provide you with the drive you need for the short-term. This is why it is not just a good practice to write down your goals, it is also a good practice to review them from time to time to keep you fired up.

One of the reasons people fail to set goals is not because they don't know how. They simply are afraid of commitment. No one likes to live with a constant reminder of their failures. *"I'm afraid I won't be able to reach my goals and I'll feel depressed for not attaining them. It is better that I don't even set them to begin with."* That line of thinking will keep you in a continuous state of running away from commitments and challenges that can to back you into a corner. For you to overcome this, and improve your self-motivation, you must learn how to zero in on your core motivation to the exclusion of distractions and mere wishes disguised as goals.

Here's an exercise you can begin to do right this moment:

Grab a pen and paper right now and write out your 20 top goals for the next 1-month period. Go ahead, stop reading and do it. When that is done, take all the time you need to carefully think about all the items on your list and pick out the 5 most important goals that you absolutely must accomplish within the next month. Write those 5 goals on a separate sheet of paper. Get to work on those 5 goals and never give your attention to any other goal until you have accomplished those 5 most important goals within the set time frame. Those 5 goals are where your core motivation lies. The remaining items on the list are distractions and mere wishes! You can get to them after you are done with your 5 most important goals if you still have the desire to accomplish these wishes.

Be Flexible

Be flexible, not just with your goals, but also with your ideologies and philosophies about what is right and wrong. Change, as we all know, is the only thing that is constant. Better ideas will appear along your path, so be willing to change. Holding tightly to ideas that no longer serve you can cause a lot of emotional upsurges which are entirely unnecessary if you understand the concept of evolution and advancement.

Be willing to step out of your comfort zone every once in a while. Challenge your ideas, your beliefs, and your opinions. That is how to grow – to improve. If and when you begin to notice emotions that don't feel good to you, ask yourself what thoughts and ideas are you holding on to that are causing you to feel the way you are feeling. Being rigid can lead to distortions in the way you think. And if your thoughts about a situation are distorted, you are more likely to have an emotional response that doesn't feel good.

With respect to goals, you need to be realistic about them. Know what you are capable of and what you wish you were capable of. And for goodness sake, if there is a major change that is definitely going to affect your attainment of the goal, be flexible enough to adjust either the time limit or the magnitude of the goal. Remember that if you beat yourself up for not meeting a goal, even though it wasn't your fault that things changed, you are sending a message to your brain that says you are a failure. That will dampen your spirit and lessen your motivation. To build self-confidence, you need to have a sense of achievement. So, adjust your goals according to prevailing changes so that when you accomplish them, you will boost your sense of achievement which in turn increases your self-confidence and sets you up for more achievements.

Seek Help and Give Help

It is a clear sign of emotional maturity to ask for help from friends, family, and colleagues when working on improving your emotional intelligence. First, it makes you accountable to someone else, and secondly, the other person will likely hold you in high regard for being so bold as to ask for their help in your pursuit of personal development.

Asking your spouse, friends, or co-workers to give you honest feedback about your behavior in different aspects will open you up to receiving lots of insights about what you need to improve upon. I must add, however, that it takes a lot of guts and maturity to do this. *"Honey, I'm working on my temper. Would you be kind enough to help me out and let me know when I'm reacting to something out of anger?"* Now that's an audacious move, but the result is worth it.

Give help to others when they need it. You can give help in various ways. Helping other people succeed in their endeavors is a great way to keep your own motivation up.

Be Approachable

What good will your emotional intelligence be if you are not approachable? How can you effectively affect others in a positive manner if there is an invisible fence around you that keeps others far away from you? Clearly, there is a huge gap that needs to be filled in your ability to show empathy if you are unapproachable.

Here's something I suggest you keep in mind especially if you lead in any capacity. Watch the people you lead and take note of how often they turn to you for moral support. If they tend to go to other people for advice, encouragement, and moral support, yet seldom approach you for any of such even though you are their leader, it is high time you double checked your empathy level.

To make yourself approachable:

- Always wear an encouraging smile. Let your smile be genuine; it will show in your eyes.

- Offer to help others even before they ask (as long as it is within reason). Every once in a while, go out of your way to offer assistance.

- Let your body language say you are approachable. Adopt a posture that is approachable when speaking with others, like placing your hands at your side. Don't fold your arms across your chest; that is an unwelcoming posture.

- Make and maintain eye contact in a friendly way.

- Keep your face open and easy to see especially when you are indoors. Wearing dark sunglasses or hats inside may obscure your face and give people a psychological message that you don't want to be approached.

- Be attentive when interacting with others. If you are constantly checking your phone or giving your attention to some other thing, they may feel they are interrupting you or that you don't want them disturbing you.

- Dress well and look appealing. If you dress to stand out, it may even be an opportunity to start up conversations when people comment about your appearance. And it goes without saying; be mindful of your hygiene. No one will enjoy approaching you if you are not clean or are unmindful of your physical appearance.

- Give sincere and honest compliments and commendations.

- Avoid gossip. Don't let yourself be known for making rude and insensitive remarks about others.

- Don't betray people's trust. If people know you can keep their secrets, they will feel comfortable approaching you, even with very confidential personal issues.

Get Social

In these days of social media, you'd think getting social would be a piece of cake, but it really isn't. First, social media is not an appropriate place to learn how to improve your people skills. There is a world of difference between texting someone and speaking to them face to face. So, when I say get social, I am not suggesting that you create more social media accounts.

Here's what I mean:

- Knock on your neighbor's door to discuss a pressing issue instead of leaving them a voice mail.

- Discuss that "hot" topic over lunch instead of texting back and forth with your friend.

- Go to your boss and express your idea face to face instead of emailing them your groundbreaking idea.

Understand that Negative Emotions Don't Make You Bad

You are not your emotions. If the emotions you feel are good or bad, it has got nothing to do with who you are. So, stop thinking you are bad because you feel bad emotions. First of all, you cannot tell your brain which chemicals to release into your body. You can only manage the effects of those chemicals – the emotions themselves. So, give up your attempts to suppress negative emotions. Let your body feel what it feels but keep your reactions under control.

Don't Be Shy About Discussing Your Feelings

Be open about how you feel. This is a sign that your EQ is on a high level. It is an error to think that people who openly talk about how they feel are weak. Don't just smile and bottle up your emotions; be willing to discuss your vulnerabilities, feelings, and thoughts.

Chapter 6: Applying Emotional Intelligence in the Workplace

Imagine for a minute that you walk into your office and find two work colleagues (let's call them Ted and Bob) in an argument while some other staffers looked on. Ted is talking animatedly and seems to have Bob and every other person in the room under his spell. Bob, on the other hand, is calmly trying to explain himself, but Ted won't have any of his explanation.

Who would you say has the outward appearance of dominating the argument? Apparently Ted, right? Now put yourself in Ted's shoes, what do you think he is feeling at that moment? Do you think he is feeling in charge or feeling frustrated and angered? Of course, he is showing his anger and frustration! Is someone who is frustrated *actually* in charge? Absolutely not! Bob, on the other hand, has the outward appearance of being weak and dominated. However, he is calm, cool, and collected. This is the hallmark of someone who is in charge – someone who is in control of the situation. Who would you rather be in this scenario: Ted or Bob?

Emotions in the Workplace

Part of what makes you a human is your capacity for emotion. You simply cannot walk into your office or workplace and switch off your emotions; they are with you every waking moment of your life. Even if an organization tries to force you to bottle up your emotions during working hours, you'll end up frustrated and unable to give your best because a part of you has been suppressed. A workplace where emotions are suppressed is a workplace full of pretense. Organizations have long realized that to get the best out of employees, they must, as a necessity, allow emotions to be expressed because employees are humans and not machines.

Even in these days of rapid technological advancements and the increased takeover of jobs from humans by machines, one thing is clear: machines don't have emotions and therefore cannot have empathy, social or people skills, or deep self-awareness. For an organization to grow, humans with emotions are still needed.

However, one of the major drawbacks with humans is that not many of us have taken the time to learn *how* to manage our emotions. This is why we allow our emotions to get out of hand in the workplace, like Ted in the scenario described above. If you let your emotions control you in the workplace, they may keep you from occupying positions that you qualify for based on your curriculum vitae, certifications, or IQ, especially supervisory, managerial, or leadership positions. As an example, would you prefer Ted to lead your marketing team, or would you rather have Bob do the job? Obviously, you would prefer someone like Bob who can get along with others on the team and be more compassionate and empathetic toward them. This is the type of person that can lead a team to achieve even the most difficult and challenging tasks. A lack of emotional intelligence can cost you great opportunities in the workplace. As a matter of fact, it can even cost you your job.

Why Emotional Intelligence Matters in the Workplace

The workplace mostly consists of teams; you work with others to achieve a common goal. And even if you run a one-man business, you still have your customers or clients to relate with. A workplace is hardly a place of isolated work. It is an environment where people with different personalities, temperaments, and IQs have to relate with each other in the pursuit of an organization's goals. This environment has to be healthy for all if the intended goals are to be achieved.

Emotional intelligence is a key ingredient for building and maintaining such a healthy working environment. If every employee were to let their emotions run the show, what you'll have will not be a workplace, but a jungle, where the strongest and fittest get to boss others around.

In a world that is fast changing, it is only wise to develop the ability to adapt to change. Emotionally intelligent people are those who are quick to adapt to change. They don't hold tight to the traditional way of doing things or performing their jobs. Employees whose EQ are on the low end of the spectrum tend to resist change at all cost.

These days it is no longer uncommon for companies to test for emotional intelligence during the hiring process. The reason is simple: they are looking for the candidates that are the most likely to blend in with existing teams. Individuals whose EQ test results show that they may cause problems to existing teams in the workplace might not be considered for employment or job opportunities.

Perhaps the following statistics from a career survey will help you see why emotional intelligence is a valuable skill to have in the workplace:

- 71% of managers valued employee's emotional quotient over their intelligence quotient.

- 75% of managers are more likely to promote workers with high emotional intelligence.

- 59% of managers are less likely to hire job seekers who possess a high IQ but low EQ (Career Builder, 2011).

The above statistics clearly show that being book smart alone is not what gives you an edge in the workplace. You need to combine your job skills with emotional skills too. Again, emotional intelligence is not just for the benefit of the organization you work for, or for the people you relate with. You are its direct and first beneficiary as it is capable of increasing your job satisfaction and also improving your job performance. Equally, if you happen to lead or manage other employees, they will share in job satisfaction because they work directly with someone whose emotional intelligence is high. And even if you are currently not in a position of managing others at work, displaying a high level of emotional intelligence puts you in a good place to be considered for elevation into leadership positions.

Emotional Intelligence Traits in the Workplace

So, what are the attributes of an employee who has high emotional intelligence? Is it when an employee is calm during an argument (like Bob) that they are said to be emotionally intelligent? Well, while displaying self-restraint is certainly a good behavior, emotional intelligence is comprised of a whole lot of other attributes.

Aside from effectively combining emotions, rational thinking, and the ability to show emotion-related behavioral restraint, here are some of the major attributes emotionally intelligent employees are known for at work:

1. Extraversion: This does not necessarily mean that all emotionally intelligent persons are extroverts. What this means is that they have developed the ability to become at ease when relating to others and are more forthcoming, irrespective of their personality traits. They don't just huddle into a corner away from their work colleagues. They relate well and freely with most (if not all) of their colleagues. Even when they are not trying to have a conversation, others feel comfortable talking with them and confiding in them or seeking their opinion, advice, or suggestions.

2. Emotional stability: They tend to have extra tolerance to work-related stress. They perform optimally even when they are under pressure. They don't freak out or lose their nerves easily. And even when things seem not to be going their way at work, they control their emotional response. You'll very rarely see them having an emotional breakdown or outburst.

3. Conscientiousness: They are diligent in performing their tasks. They painstakingly dedicate their time and energy to bring out the best in themselves and others without nitpicking or micromanaging.

4. Self-efficacy: Emotionally intelligent employees tend to have a high level of confidence in their ability to effectively handle, manage, and cope with whatever rigorous demands come with their jobs.

Major Areas of Application

Although emotional intelligence can be applied to virtually all aspects of work life, there are three major areas where its impact can be most felt in the workplace.

These are:

1. Leadership: Have you noticed that organizations with emotionally robust leadership tend to have an equally robust workforce? It is interesting to note how positivity influences and impacts others further down the ladder. This is evidently so because leaders and managers who demonstrate a high level of emotional intelligence have the capacity to:

- Positively influence those they lead using inspirational and motivational talks. They have developed their ability to be persuasive without coming across as being bossy.

- Clearly and effectively communicate their purpose to the people they lead. This clarity of purpose makes every person on their team catch on to the vision and mission they have.

- Put a leash on their behavioral responses to their own emotions, and also help those they lead to identify and manage their emotions as well.

- Respond appropriately to situations that are capable of causing disorder, stress, and bad energy in the workplace.

    2. **Project management**: Supervisors, unit heads, and team leaders who are in charge of smaller projects and are in direct contact with the majority of their colleagues need a high level of emotional intelligence to be able to perform optimally. Their daily interaction levels and handling of peer-heavy projects puts them in a position where emotional intelligence skills must be brought to bear. Project managers are expected to recognize and tactfully influence emotional responses from their peers, in order to accomplish projects to specification and as scheduled. They must possess the ability to control their expression of emotions as well as steer

individual project members away from potential problems. When different project supervisors and unit heads with a high level of emotional intelligence are able to coordinate their teams, then an organization with a productive workforce is born.

3. **Social work**: Those whose jobs fall under the category of social work are saddled with the greatest challenge of demonstrating emotional intelligence. Social work requires a high level of empathy (compassion) and an ample dose of self-motivation. It doesn't matter if the social work is done in a hospital, day care facility, prison, human resources department, foster care agency, or in a school environment, the demands are practically the same. There is a higher level of emotional challenge involved in that line of work. A high level of emotional intelligence must be demonstrated in order to:

- Properly observe and assess clients.

- Know the best approach to adopt when engaging different clients.

- Enlist cooperation and collaboration.

- Properly handle stress.

- Effectively make decisions without bias, prejudice, or fear.

The application of emotional intelligence in these three core areas (leadership, project management, and social work) ensures efficiency, effectiveness, and higher productivity in the workplace.

Lack of Emotional Intelligence in the Workplace: The Negative Impact

Now, let us shift our focus to consider the negative impact a lack of emotional intelligence can have in the workplace. Broadly speaking, a lack of emotional intelligence can result in communication breakdown or poor communication, and it can also have a negative impact on decision-making.

Poor communication

Efficiency and productivity in the workplace are intricately tied to effective communication. Take a moment to picture an organization or a team where the employees, managers, or team members:

- Don't have an adequate understanding of their emotions.

- Can't really read between the lines to figure out the emotions of their colleagues, subordinates, and supervisors.

- Don't know how to properly communicate their feelings, so that they are always expressing themselves through emotional outbursts, holding back important information, or giving out too much information.

Such an organization or team is definitely going to have less productivity due to poor communication.

Decision-making

Decision-making is usually accompanied by some strong emotions such as anxiety and fear, especially when the decision is likely to have a significant impact on the organization. When the person or group of persons saddled with the responsibility of decision-making lacks a high level of emotional intelligence, they may not be able to manage their emotional state of mind which may lead them to make decisions that involve too many risks or too few risks.

A Few Practical Examples

The workplace is comprised of people from different backgrounds, therefore, it is expected that issues and problems will arise due to the differences in views, perceptions, understanding, and of course, emotional quotient level. If these issues are not handled in the most appropriate manner, it can escalate into bigger problems.

I can go on and on about how important emotional intelligence is in the workplace, but without giving practical examples of how these things are applicable in a workplace situation, all that talk will amount to abstract and vague discussions. So, let us consider a few practical examples of both high and low demonstrations of emotional intelligence in the workplace.

Example 1

You discover that your team cannot possibly complete a project within the time required. The project is very crucial to you, the company, and the public.

You are faced with the following options:

- Decide to pressure your team to complete the project at all cost (longer hours, working harder). Will this help their motivation or frustrate them?

- Choose to move back the deadline to give your team more time to complete the project. Will that tell your team that you can be pushed around? How will the company and public react to the postponement? Will that protect your self-image?

- Discipline the team for the delay. Will this encourage the team to give their best? Will team members who gave their best not feel bad for taking the fall for someone else's shortcomings?

- Discipline the individuals responsible for the project delay. Will this foster team spirit?

- Encourage them to put in their best. Will this motivate them, or will you be setting a precedent for accommodating excuses for failure?

How do you demonstrate emotional intelligence in this situation? Rushing your team to forcefully complete the project (out of panic) may lead to improper project execution, distrust from the public, and a disgruntled team.

One excellent way to handle this will be to do as suggested below:

1. First, take a deep breath to calm and steady yourself. You and every other person on the team are obviously under

serious pressure to deliver. Recognize that the pressure is causing a lot of emotions to run wild inside of you. Breathing will help you regain composure before making any decision.

2. Come up with a convincing explanation or work with the PR unit to come up with a campaign to convince the public why the project needs to be delayed.

3. Reframe the situation to make all involved (the company and public) see that the delay will bring about a positive change that will make the project even better.

4. Speak with your team to motivate them. Reassure them and make them know they have your support.

5. Take the time to speak with the individuals that may have caused the delay. Let them know that they are not failures and that they can ask for help anytime they need it. Do your best to boost their psychological state of mind.

6. Get everyone back to work and ensure you show them adequate moral support to help them meet the new deadline.

Example 2

One of your subordinates walks into your office and starts to criticize another work colleague behind their back. It is obvious to you that both employees have been arguing, but you don't know what the difference in view is about. To make the matter even more delicate, both of the employees involved are excellent at performing their duties.

You are faced with the following choices:

- Agree with the criticism and even join in on criticizing the other employee. Will the other employee see you as a competent manager?

- Decide to caution or discipline the employee who is being criticized. Will that be fair to the other employee?

- Decide to discipline or caution the employee who is criticizing the other. Will this drive the employee away from you or draw them closer?

- Choose to get involved in the argument yourself. Will your view help to end the argument?

- Decide to ignore the criticism and argument, with the hope that it will die off naturally, or allow the two of them to work things out themselves. Will this approach work to solve the issue or will it allow it to escalate?

- Decide to dig further to understand the point of argument between the two employees. Should you speak to them individually or at the same time? Should you involve other employees in this issue? Will this be a judicious use of your time or a waste of time?

How do you tackle this situation using your emotional intelligence? Threatening both employees may not result in any positive outcome even if it does handle the immediate issue. That is like a temporal bandage for a long-term issue, plus it shows a lack of emotional intelligence on your part.

A good way to demonstrate your adept emotional skills would be to:

1. Gather information from all parties involved by asking appropriate questions.

2. Be a mediator between the two employees without appearing to take sides.

3. See if both could state their own intent clearly so that you can eliminate assumptions that led to the argument and criticism.

4. Point out the misunderstanding and make it clear that neither intended to hurt the other's feelings.

5. Get both to apologize to each other and return to work.

Example 3

Bob's work colleague is moody and it is affecting their productivity. They are having a bad day at work.

Here's how to know if Bob has low emotional intelligence:

1. If he ignores the moody colleague or doesn't even notice that his colleague is in a bad mood in spite of the fact that he has been interacting with them all day.

2. If Bob criticizes or makes comments to make the moody colleague feel worse, like "snap out of it!"

And here's how to know if Bob has high emotional intelligence:

1. He notices that something is eating up his colleague and he asks questions and offers a listening ear.

2. He tries to cheer them up.

3. He directs their attention to the good things happening for them even when some things aren't going as planned.

4. He tries to distract them from their present worries.

Example 4

One of your best employees asks for a pay raise. You are very well aware of the high value this employee brings to your company. The problem, however, is that you cannot afford to increase their pay right now.

You are faced with the following choices:
- Decide to keep the employee happy and motivated by increasing their pay. Will that salary increment affect the company negatively? What message will you be passing to other employees who are equally good?

- Decide to be straightforward and say no. Will that dampen the employee's morale? Will they begin to seek employment somewhere else where they can get better pay?

- Offer them other options aside from money. Will they settle for something other than money?

- Explain why a pay raise is not feasible at the moment. Will they understand? Will they also reduce their performance pending such time as when they can get a pay raise?

In what way will you handle this situation that can show a high level of emotional intelligence? This is a very sensitive issue that must be handled carefully because the way you handle this situation could mean the difference between keeping and losing a very valuable employee.

Here's a good suggestion:

1. Whatever you do, and even if the employee is not as valuable as they thought they were, do not say no straight away. You may be inclined to say a straightforward no especially under a very strict budget, but, resist that temptation. A direct no will send a clear message to the employee that you do not value their input and that is one sure way to make them start looking elsewhere.

2. Create a welcoming atmosphere conducive for the employee to discuss freely with you why they think they should get a pay raise. Dig deep to learn how long they

have wanted the salary increase and what they will do if they don't get it right away. Also, ensure that your discussion remains private. You do not want other employees to begin to bombard you with a pay raise request.

3. Get them to see other alternatives aside from a pay raise. Calmly explain to them why you cannot afford to increase their salary at the moment. Do not dodge the "yes" or "no" answer. Instead, you can say "yes, but" and proceed to explain the reason for the "*but*". Another way to put this is to say, "*Yes, but not right now.*" Or "*I can offer you this and this for now until our finances improve.*"

Example 5

A meeting is turning into a war of words. People are beginning to shout others down and tempers are boiling hot.

To know if someone has a low level of emotional intelligence, simply look at those in the shouting match. Anyone banging their fist on the desk, frantically pointing fingers at others, and trying to get everyone to agree to their point of view is probably the most deficient in emotional intelligence.

On the other hand, here's how to spot a person who has worked on their emotional intelligence. They tend to:

- Remain calm during meetings.

- Allow others to table their views.

- Pay close attention and practice attentive listening skills.

- Not interrupt when others are speaking.

Testing Potential Employees for Emotional Intelligence

One of the best places to apply emotional intelligence skills is in the human resources department of an organization. When candidates are tested for emotional intelligence before being given job opportunities, it increases the chances of having a vibrant working environment. Moreover, when candidates applying for a particular position appear to all have qualifications and certifications that are at par, testing their emotional intelligence will help you narrow down the best candidates for the position.

There are several tests you can use to measure a candidate's emotional intelligence. Nevertheless, here are a few tips to keep in mind:

1. Call the references for each candidate. Don't simply rely on a reference letter – they are not detailed enough. Ask the candidates' references questions that can unearth their general attitudes especially as it relates to treating others.

2. Avoid tests that are based on self-reporting. It can lead to inappropriate reporting, as some candidates may exaggerate their emotional abilities. It is also possible to have candidates who are not self-aware enough to give an accurate self-report.

3. Do not use personality tests for emotional intelligence tests. A personality test may show what a candidate's

major traits are, but it does not show development needs.

4. Do not use a test tool that is designed based on reports from others (for example, a 360-degree feedback tool).

5. Ask follow-up questions aimed at verifying responses.

Example of Interview Questions Targeted at Emotional Behavior

Let's bring this chapter to a close by taking a look at a few good interview questions that can help you determine the emotional intelligence level of a candidate.

First things first, make sure that the atmosphere is warm and welcoming. Your aim is to get the candidate in a frame of mind that is as comfortable as possible so that you can get them to freely share the information you seek. Do not make it feel like an inquisition; a friendly atmosphere should be your goal.

1. Start by asking the usual questions about their background, education, and depth of experience.

2. Ask the candidate to share a story of when they were involved in a situation that was challenging. Ask them to give you a brief highlight of how they led or helped others to successfully overcome the challenge.

3. Next, ask them to go into details about the event. Be sure to ask how they felt and what they thought during those times, what specifically they did that resulted in success.

4. Now ask them to share another story of how they were faced with a challenging situation but failed to overcome the challenge. Ask what valuable lessons they learned from the situation and the failure.

This line of questioning will give you clear insights into their strengths, weaknesses, whether they are self-aware enough or not, their empathy level, as well as their motivation level. You will now be able to determine if they can work well with others in your organization.

Bottom Line

The fact is that even though you can boost your career by acquiring certifications in various pursuits, you cannot get a certification in emotional intelligence. Emotional intelligence is something you must personally work to improve on a continuous basis.

Chapter 7: Applying Emotional Intelligence in Personal Relationships

Emotional intelligence has nice sounding academic definitions and is very easy to master on the pages of a book. But when it comes to real-life, down-to-earth practical application, especially when it involves the people who are closest to us, it is a different ballgame entirely. It seems as if we tend to exercise more self-restraint when we are dealing with outsiders (at work, in business interactions, and so on) than we do when we are dealing with the people that matter most to us.

A typical example can be seen between siblings. It is not uncommon to witness siblings griping and whining over things that they normally wouldn't do with others. Even when they have grown into adults and have each improved their respective levels of emotional intelligence; once they come together, they tend to "let down their guards" and fall back into old argumentative habits.

It doesn't matter if you like a person or not, if you work in the same place, you are obliged to relate with them in one way or another. However, this is not always so with personal relationships. You can decide to call it quits with the other person if the personal relationship is not working. Even in parent-child relationships, either party can decide to estrange themselves from the other, especially when there are unresolved conflicts.

To maintain love and camaraderie in friendships, family, and romantic relationships, it is important for at least one person in the relationship to have a good level of emotional intelligence.

Unmet Emotional Needs

One of the major factors that leads to an unhappy relationship (whether romantic, friendship or parent-child relationship) is an accumulation of unmet emotional needs.

Here's exactly what I mean: your level of care and interest in your partner shows how much you value the relationship. When your partner says they feel a certain way, you would like to know why they feel that way and if there is something you can do to either make them feel better (if it is a bad feeling) or increase that feeling (if it is a good one). This is the ideal way things happen in a relationship that is valued by both partners. One or both of them have their emotional needs met, therefore, it is easier to maintain and enjoy such a valued relationship.

On the other hand, if you have emotional needs that are not met in a relationship, it becomes difficult to value that relationship. For example, if you are feeling unappreciated by your spouse, it is difficult for you to show them that you care about how their boss isn't valuing their input at work. Your natural instinct is to first care for yourself before another. You simply cannot offer what you do not have.

In a relationship, especially a romantic relationship, where one or both partners have a lot of unmet emotional needs, there is a high chance of violent outburst, unchecked reactions, and a lot of hurt feelings. These are all signs that emotional intelligence is lacking in that relationship.

It is true that your happiness doesn't depend on anyone, but of what use is being in a relationship if all you get is a feeling of being hurt? Relationships are supposed to be for the mutual benefit of the parties involved, which is why a lot of trust is invested in relationships – trust that the other person will care, empathize and be interested in the things that matter to you. Therefore, once that trust is breached it causes emotional pain. The pain can show up as anger, hurt, or sadness. If the pain continues for a considerable amount of time, it diminishes the value the partner feeling the pain has for the relationship and may even cause them to call it quits.

While it is not possible to please other people 100% of the time, being in a relationship requires that you develop extra sensitivity to the other person's needs, especially emotional ones. That is why empathy – the emotional skill of putting yourself in another person's shoes – is very important to develop in a relationship. Your partner wants to feel cared for just like you do too. It is your show of care (empathy) that tells your partner how valuable they (and the relationship) are to you. The more you make them feel important by meeting their emotional needs, the more valuable they will feel to you. And the more valuable they feel, the more they will want to make you feel valuable too. It is a win-win situation for all.

Letting Others Off the Hook

As mentioned earlier, no one is responsible for your happiness; not even the most romantic partner in the world that you can find, or your best friend. Emotionally intelligent people recognize this fact and they do not go into a relationship with the intent of placing the responsibility of their happiness on someone else's shoulders.

Here's how to know a partner is low on emotional intelligence and has placed their happiness on the other person. They say things like, "You hurt me." But what should one say if they are feeling hurt in a relationship? Well, it's not an easy thing to remember, but practicing self-regulation on a continuous basis will help you to pick your words carefully so that you don't put the other partner on the defensive. Instead of attacking or blaming the other person when you feel hurt, you can simply inform them about how you feel. An emotionally intelligent response would be, "I feel hurt." It not easy to remember, but it is doable. Saying things like this means you are letting the other person off the hook and merely giving them information. You cannot force them to do anything about the information, but at least you have let them know how you feel. Demanding that they do something about the information is also immature or (in the context of this book) low on emotional intelligence. In other words, you are putting the responsibility of feeling happy on your partner – which is an exercise in futility.

Your best bet is to simply relay the information about how you feel to your partner and leave it up to them to choose what to do about it. Don't try to manipulate people to do as you please, nor should you make them feel guilty for not empathizing with you when you feel you need it.

You see, the worst time you can ever seek empathy is when you are in dire need of it. If you are already hurting and then you try to become important to someone else in a bid to get empathy from them or for them to soothe your pain, you are more likely to become annoyed at them if they don't give you enough attention. You may end up pushing them away with your blaming and attacking. No one can show empathy when they are on the defensive.

Saying, "You don't care about me!" when you need your partner to empathize with you is going to get you nowhere. And even if you do get an immediate favorable response, that response is not genuine and may not be sustained because it is a forced response. In all probability, the immediate favorable response is likely to have been prompted by a feeling of guilt which you evoked in the other person.

The point here is simple: it is counterproductive and a brazen display of low emotional intelligence to blame and attack another person when what you want from them is empathy.

To demonstrate your mastery of emotions, you should:

- Express your feelings in a way that does not attack the other person.

- Ensure that you are aware of the emotions you are evoking in the other person.

Using your emotional skills in a healthy manner will generate a feeling of positivity in your partner. Conversely, resentment is likely to be the result if you use your emotional skills to generate negativity in your partner. An accumulation of negative feelings could be very toxic to the relationship.

The Importance of Identifying Your Emotions

One of the key elements you will come across as you study emotional intelligence is to identify your emotions. It seems obvious but in reality, most people don't identify their emotions. For example, a person may feel angered by the behavior of their partner and think that anger is the primary emotion they are feeling. But anger is a secondary emotion; there is a primary emotion causing the anger. If you cannot identify that emotion, you may be shouting into the wind!

To identify the primary emotion underneath the anger, ask yourself, what is making me angry at this moment? Am I feeling unappreciated, disrespected, attacked, or pressured? It is the intense feeling of these things that eventually leads to anger. It is like having road rage: the driver is expressing anger as a result of an underlying frustration, rejection, hurt, or some other intense feeling. All those feelings are lying beneath the surface, leaving only the anger to show up like an iceberg.

When you are able to identify your primary emotions, you are in a better position to deal with them. Here's a scenario that may help you in identifying your emotions. This example uses the ability to recognize patterns.

Let us assume Jane is having a difficult time in her marriage because she is not feeling appreciated. She often feels annoyed by her husband and she is gradually transferring that irksomeness into the way she relates with her kids. She's trying to figure out why she is so easily annoyed even when the kids mean no harm. Jane takes out a pen and a paper and decides to write down incidences of the times she felt strongly annoyed at her husband.

She remembers:

- Her husband failing to thank her for being helpful to him the other day, even when it wasn't convenient for her to do so.

- Her husband criticizing her for not being very helpful even though she did her best.

- Her husband not acknowledging her sincere compliments.

As Jane writes down these things, she begins to recognize a pattern. In all the cases, she was not appreciated. So, her primary emotion is that she is feeling unappreciated and that is causing her to feel irked at both her husband and anything that reminds her of him (including the kids!).

Now Jane can get to work on the right emotion. She has identified her unmet emotional needs – appreciation. It becomes simpler to deal directly with that.

Handling Identified Negative Emotions

There are several ways to handle negative emotions that have been clearly identified. It depends on a lot of factors such as the type of relationship, how deeply involved or committed the partners are, and so on. Let me briefly highlight the general guidelines that can guide you on handling negative emotions skillfully.

1. First of all, you need to identify the primary emotion as Jane did in the scenario above.

2. Now tell the other partner how you feel. Remember not to frame your statement in an attacking manner like "You don't appreciate me." Say something like, "I feel unappreciated" or whatever it is you are feeling. Never put the blame on the other partner. They are never responsible for how you feel because your emotions are ultimately yours; they emanate from you.

3. Notice the response of your partner.

4. Keep a close watch on how you feel about their response. Remember, you are seeking ways to manage or handle your own negative emotions. You are not on a hunt for whom to blame for your feelings. However, their response will tell you how valuable the relationship is to them.

5. Decide if you can keep giving more of yourself to the relationship or not.

6. In the case where you recognize that this is not the first relationship you are having this same emotional issue with, then perhaps you need to dig deep within yourself and work on how best to tackle your emotional needs.

Signs of Low Emotional Intelligence in a Relationship

Generally, a breakdown in communication is a sign that a relationship lacks emotional intelligence or at least one partner needs to work on their emotional skills. However, miscommunication can show up in several different ways. A relationship that has the following signs clearly needs urgent emotional improvement:

- Assuming that the other partner should know their intentions. When one or both partners resort to signaling their emotional intentions in the false hope that the other should "read in between the lines," they are leaving room for misunderstanding, frustration, and resentment.

- Emotionally blackmailing the other partner is a sign of emotional immaturity. When one or both partners resort to sulking, giving the silent treatment, or trying to make the other person feel guilty, they clearly need to work on their communication.

- Neediness and attention-seeking behaviors are also a sign that one or both partners are confusing love with need.

Unfortunately, a lot of relationships have one or more of the above elements. When effective communication is lacking in a relationship, it simply means those in the relationship are afraid the other person won't accept them and love them as they truly are.

It is an error to conclude that when couples have arguments or conflicts, they have low emotional intelligence. That is not necessarily true as they may be in the process of learning how to work on their emotional intelligence. Also, it is not the arguments and conflicts that happen between couples that matter. What matters most is the manner of the argument, and how they are able to resolve the conflicts. That is to say, it is not *what* they argue about that matters, but *how* they go about arguing – maturely or immaturely.

EI Activities for Couples

The following activities are carefully designed to help improve emotional intelligence in couples. However, bear in mind that the task of developing your emotional intelligence takes time and effort. Also, you will need exposure to real-life situations in order to put what you have learned into practice. But not to worry, there are lots of opportunities to practice your emotional skills especially if you are in a relationship. All you need is patience and consistency. It will be helpful if you get your partner in on the show. Let them understand that you are working on yourself and on improving the relationship you share with them. They will most likely join you in the learning process.

Here are some great activities that both of you can practice:

Activity 1: Explain your intentions

This activity is aimed at explaining exactly what you mean to your partner when you act in ways that seem threatening to them and the relationship. Your intentions when you behave in certain ways may be clear to you, however, your partner likely does not have the gift of mind reading, so they may not know your intentions. This activity will help to clarify your intentions to them.

1. For this activity, get a piece of paper and draw two columns.

2. Label the first column as "Miscommunications" and directly under that, write the words, "When I…"

3. Write your name at the top of the second column and directly under that, write the words, "My intention is…"

4. Now fill the first column with the behaviors that seem threatening to your partner. For example, your first column may have things like: "give you the silent treatment," "get mad at you," and "nag you."

5. Fill the second column with your intentions. For example, your second column may have things like: "I am feeling lonely" or "I need your attention" and so on. Taking the first line of the above, your statement will be: *"When I… give you the silent treatment, my intention is… I am feeling lonely."*

6. Make sure to fill both columns with as many of your behaviors as you feel your partner needs to understand.

7. Let your partner follow the same steps as above

8. Now exchange the lists you have written with your partner. This may lead to more open communication between you.

Activity 2: Question Time

This activity is in the form of holding an interview with your partner. You both take turns to ask similar questions with the aim of digging into their past to see how communication styles they grew up with could be affecting their current communication style.

Whatever your discovery about your partner's past or upbringing, keep in mind that the goal of this activity is never to try to change your partner. Rather, it is intended to help you understand where they are coming from. It may be desirable to get them to improve some aspects of their lives, but never force them to change. Remember also that even if they are willing to make changes, it will take time. The fact that they are willing to commit to the process of improving themselves should be enough respite for you. What they need from you is your support and encouragement. Notice even the slightest improvement in their behavior and praise it. It shows them that you care about their progress and that their effort is not lost on you.

Take turns with your partner to ask and honestly answer the following questions:

1. Who were your role models as a child?

2. Were your parents or guardians open when they communicate / how would you describe your parent's communication style?

3. When your parents became upset, how did they behave toward each other?

4. When you got angry, were you allowed to express your feelings, or were you told it is bad to express your feelings, especially when they were negative ones?

Come up with any other questions you feel might be helpful in your own particular relationship. When you ask these questions, practice active listening. Do not interrupt your partner when they are answering or explaining something to you. Give them your undivided attention and encourage them through nods and direct eye contact to show that you understand what they are telling you. Be honest and open when answering the questions as this will also encourage your partner to do the same.

This activity may uncover how your partner was treated when he or she was a kid, and how he or she has grown with that treatment ingrained in their minds. If a child was not given enough airtime to voice their feelings or a sufficient listening ear when they expressed themselves, they may take that communication into their future relationships.

Keep These in Mind

Let me share some quick tips that will be of immense benefit to those who are in any kind of personal relationship. Remembering and applying these things will make you stand out as someone who is emotionally skilled:

1. There is a thin line between emotions and beliefs. The way you think about your emotions is quite different from what those emotions are. One – the emotions – unite you and your partner; the other – your belief – is capable of causing separation.

2. It is not possible to be empathetic when feeling defensive. Therefore, do not attack your partner.

3. Avoid trying to defend your feelings. Always remember that it is pointless trying to debate feelings. All it does is put the other person on the defensive.

4. When you invalidate the other person's feelings or judge them too quickly, you may end up destroying that relationship.

5. The emotionally intelligent partner in a relationship is the one who stays calm. The one who gets annoyed and irritated is most likely the one who needs empathy. He or she carries a lot of unmet emotional needs, is placing their responsibility on another person, or has a long way to go as far as emotional intelligence is concerned.

6. Do not employ sarcasm when expressing yourself. It belies hurt, bitterness, and hostility. Learn to be assertive without being rude when expressing your feelings to your partner.

7. Using your partner's words against them is a very hurtful way to attack them. They may never get over it.

8. Don't force the other person to agree with your explanation or view. Explaining your feelings to someone who is not interested is wasted effort.

9. First, try to understand your partner, then try to make yourself understood.

10. The partner who has an emotional wound is not likely to listen to logic. Quit trying to soothe their pain with logic.

11. You should not assume when it comes to how your partner feels. Always ask them how they feel. Assumptions can be fatal mistakes.

12. Always ask how your partner would feel before you make decisions. It is a mark of respect for their feelings.

13. Always say "I feel..." when you are expressing how you feel. Avoid statements that will bring your partner under attack or make them feel guilty for how you feel.

Chapter 8: How to Measure Your EQ

So, how do you measure your EQ? How do you know where you stand on the emotional intelligence scale?

Today, we live in a world of plentiful online tests. However, you need to know exactly what it is you should be looking for before you rush into taking any old EQ test. Although there is an abundance of EQ tests online, not all of them are made equally. This chapter will uncover exactly what you need to look out for when measuring your emotional intelligence. But first, why do we need to measure our emotional intelligence to begin with?

Importance of Measuring Emotional Intelligence

Here are a few key reasons why measuring your level of emotional intelligence is vital to your success. Remember, that success, as we mentioned in chapter 4, does not depend only on how high your IQ is. For you to be truly successful, you need to determine where you stand on the emotional intelligence scale, regardless of your IQ score.

It helps relationships

Relationships, whether personal or professional, are defined as the coming together of two or more persons for shared interests. It can be sustained if the individuals in the relationship have high levels of emotional intelligence. However, since it is not feasible for everyone in every relationship to become aware of their level of emotional intelligence, the one party in the relationship who takes it upon themselves to measure their own emotional intelligence is more likely to be ready and willing to make that relationship last longer. It opens you up to areas you need to work on to make your relationship with your spouse, children, colleagues, and friends better.

It can be used to predict how a person will perform

High academic performance and high job performance are good factors that can get you ahead in an academic environment or in the workplace. However, an unbiased assessment of emotional intelligence can be a determining factor for hiring people who seem to be at par on the IQ scale. You see, the workplace has changed over the years, and merely possessing a high IQ just won't cut it these days. Employers need someone who can work with others, carry others along, and understand how others think and feel. All this is because employers and business owners have figured out that a happy and highly motivated workforce is required to make a business successful, and not just people with high cognitive abilities. So yes, organizations measure your emotional intelligence through aptitude tests to know whether you are emotionally fit for the job.

It improves leadership

Leadership at all levels needs a high level of emotional intelligence. If you occupy any leadership position at home, school, or in the workplace – supervisory role, executive role, departmental head, team leader, or a coordinator of some sort – it is important to bring your emotional intelligence level up to speed, not just as a one-time event but as a continuous process. Your leadership style has to be seen as transformational leadership, where you are focused on improving the engagement behavior of the individuals you lead, as well as measuring your leadership effectiveness from the feedback you get from your followers.

Results can be improved upon

Measuring your level of emotional intelligence is like testing the knowledge level of a child before admitting them into a new class. You'll want to determine the correct class to place them in. The result of their test does not mean they cannot perform better; it only tells the teacher where to begin teaching from. Whatever the result of your emotional intelligence test, it is an indication of how you have performed so far and not an indication of your highest level of emotional performance. What your result shows is your current "class" and the "syllabus" or "curriculum" which you need to be working with to ensure that you improve beyond the current level. Without testing your emotional intelligence, you may be taking a "course" that is too advanced or too low for your current level.

The Purpose of Emotional Intelligence Tests

In essence, EQ assessment tools or tests are a series of questions designed to uncover how an individual reacts or responds to different situations. The questions are tailored to cover situations like:

- Frustrating and very stressful situations – to determine how easily turned off or annoyed you can be.

- Handling cultural sensitivity and diversity – to determine how sensitive you are about other people's points of view.

- Discouraging situations such as facing failure – to determine your level of self-motivation.

- Handling emotions in other people, especially people of varying ages – to determine how well you connect with others.

- Handling leadership roles – to determine how you manage people.

- Measuring different personality traits in other people – to determine how well you read and understand people.

When these factors have been determined, a score is generated known as the emotional quotient (EQ) score. EQ scores between 90 and 100 are considered average scores, while an EQ score of 160 is considered perfect. However, these scores are not unchangeable. Emotional intelligence can be learned and improved upon. If your EQ score is average or below average, you can improve it by:

- Deliberately engaging in activities that are capable of increasing how good you feel, which in turn reduces your level of negative feelings.

- Quickly recovering from adverse situations instead of spending time in self-pity and discouragement.

- Freely letting your intimate emotions show in personal relationships. Do not bottle up intimate emotions; they can lead to frustration and a feeling of loneliness. Intimate emotions are your basic human desire to connect to another human. Express them freely within the confines of personal relationships.

- Channel out difficult emotions when the need arises. Don't hold them in. Be assertive and develop the habit of calmly expressing yourself even in difficult situations. Develop the habit of journaling; naming and writing down your emotions and how you feel is another way of channeling the emotions.

EQ Assessment Tools

There are several tools you can use to assess your EQ level. These tools include questionnaires and quizzes specifically targeted at eliciting the right answers from test takers. By right answers, I do not mean giving responses of how things should be, but instead, how they actually are. For example, a quiz may ask test takers to respond with "Not At All", "Sometimes", or "Very Often" to the question "*I am quick to lose my temper under frustrating situations.*" The right response for each individual taking the test will vary depending on their own personal experience. So, keep in mind that when you take any EQ test, you are not required to respond with the best response that suits the question, but with exactly how you will act in the situation stated in the question. Remember, it is not a test of your IQ, but a test of your EQ.

EQ tests are broadly grouped into different tests that measure emotional intelligence based on the following criteria:

- Trait-based tests (like BarOn EQ-i)
- Behavior-based tests (like Genos)
- Competency-based tests (like ESCI)
- Ability-based tests (like MSCEIT)

These tools/tests can be accessed online. Some of the more popular tools that can give you accurate assessments include:

1. **Revenue BarOn EQ-i**: This takes into consideration the tolerance level, problem-solving ability, happiness level, stress level, and general awareness of the test

taker. It is a type of self-report test designed to measure the ability of the individual in getting along with demands and pressures from the environment.

2. **Mind Tools 15-question assessment**: This test is fast, easy, and direct to the point. It may not be very detailed, but it gives you a general idea of where you stand on the EQ scale.

3. **ECI – Emotional Competency Inventory**: This test is based on a self-assessment questionnaire that clearly shows test-takers their EQ ratings based on how they utilize their emotional abilities under varying situations.

4. **Psychology Today 146-question assessment**: This consists of test questions that are designed to ensure accuracy in assessment by asking questions in multiple ways. The test takes approximately 45 minutes and is very comprehensive.

5. **SASQ – Seligman Attributional Style Questionnaire**: This is especially developed to evaluate the pessimism and optimism levels of test takers.

6. **Talent Smart 28-question assessment**: Taking this test requires that you pay a fee. Besides determining your EQ score, this tool will further help you with strategies that you can use to improve your emotional intelligence.

7. **Institute for Health and Human Potential 17-question assessment**: This tool was designed by researchers who understand what it takes to perform under serious pressure. The test questions will give you

insights into your ability to hone in on your emotional skills.

8. **MEIS – Multifactor Emotional Intelligence Scale**: This is an ability-based test designed to evaluate the individual's ability to recognize, comprehend, and appropriately utilize their emotions.

EQ Measures

Generally, there are 3 major ways emotional intelligence can be measured. These are:

1. Self-report measure
2. Other-report measure
3. Ability measure

Remember also that there is no one particular correct answer to any question on the various EQ assessment tests. The EQ score is arrived at by analyzing answers from hundreds of responses to determine what constitutes a high, average, and low score. For example, if your response to the question "*I easily get discouraged*" is "*Disagree,*" that response (along with all of your other responses to the rest of the test questions) will be compared to hundreds of other responses from other test takers to determine what your EQ score is.

Keep in mind that these tests are not created equally. Perhaps after examining each of these EQ measures, you'll discover for yourself which measure best suits your particular situation.

Self-Report Measure

Tests that are based on self-report are great for measuring things like personality traits. They can also be used to determine if a person is happy, depressed, anxious, and so on.

However, this type of test has some serious flaws. Perhaps you are familiar with the Latin phrase, "*Nemo judex in causa sua.*" It is a principle of natural justice which, when translated to English, means "*no one should be a judge in his own case.*" Why? Bias, of course! This is one major flaw with this type of test. Test takers may respond in a way that is socially desirable instead of answering truthfully.

Again, how sufficiently aware is the test taker of his or her emotional abilities? Most people assume that they know their emotional abilities but in reality, that is far from correct. If a person does not fully understand his or her emotional abilities, their responses will definitely not be accurate.

Other-Report Measure

This type of test allows other people to assess you and give their opinions about your level of emotional intelligence. It is like asking your colleagues or friends and family to give your feedback, only this is done as a standardized test rather than merely requesting a friend's opinion about you.

It stands to reason that since emotional intelligence has a lot to do with the ability to display your people skills, it makes sense to have tests designed to get honest reports about you from other people. So, a test that uses this method of assessment will most likely involve giving out forms to your colleagues, friends, associates, and so on to fill out some information about you.

Let's take a look at a few of the questions and responses this type of test may contain.

1. Mr. X manages his emotions very well
Disagree / Agree / Maybe

2. Mr. X is able to easily connect with others
Disagree / Agree / Maybe

3. Mr. X expresses himself clearly
Disagree / Agree / Maybe

This type of test is very good at providing useful information about how others see you. You can use this information to improve your management skills, as well as to get a better handle on your use of social skills.

However, with regard to providing information about your level of emotional intelligence, this is a rather poor test type to use. The reasons are not too difficult to figure out.

First of all, the people who are giving their opinions about you are merely saying what they think about you based on the aspects of you that they know. Only you know exactly what you are capable of or not. Assuming one of the respondents chooses to rate you low on all or most of the questions on the test, does that mean your emotional intelligence level is low? If the responses are anything to go by, then you are certainly low on emotional intelligence. However, every person responding to the questions has some form of bias about you – negative or positive – which will definitely influence their responses. Also, it is possible that some of the respondents simply don't like you! No good rating can come from any such persons, no matter how good your performance is.

Secondly, if the persons responding to the questions enjoy some form of benefit from you, it will be difficult to get them to give honest feedback. For example, your students, children, employees, or dependents may not want to respond in such a way that will hurt you, even if they know that your emotional rating should be low. Even when these tests are conducted anonymously, a person who is under you is likely to praise you.

Ability Measure

Emotional intelligence is comprised of several skills such as interpersonal or social skill, self-motivation, ability to react intelligently and quickly, and the capacity to mentor others, among other skills. The best way to measure skills is by using ability tests. Tests designed based on other-report and self-report may not provide truthful and relevant information to determine an accurate EQ assessment, or any useful information as far as emotional intelligence is concerned.

A test designed based on the ability measure may have a question such as:

You openly scolded your teenage daughter in front of her friends and peers. How is she likely to feel?

Happy	Disagree / Agree / Maybe
Sad	Disagree / Agree / Maybe
Indifferent	Disagree / Agree / Maybe
Angry	Disagree / Agree / Maybe

Although there is no one best answer to this test question, there are some answers that are better than others based on the ways in which hundreds of others have answered the question, allowing a score to be determined.

This is a more accurate way to determine an individual's emotional ability under the situations outlined in the test questions.

Work on Improving These

Your EQ test score should spur you to work more on the following areas:

- **Improving your self-awareness level**. Life is not stagnant; it is a journey of discoveries. So, don't stop discovering who you are. A year from now, you may discover that what seemed to be your weakness in times past is now an area of strength for you. This means you will have to change your approach to that aspect of your life. If you take an EQ test today and take the score as a once in a lifetime result, you probably will never grow beyond your current test result.

- **Hanging onto the past**. Letting go of the past allows you to reach for more in the present moment. Do not let your past reactions to your emotions define you. For example, *"I am an ill-tempered person"* may be the honest result of your self-awareness assessment. However, do not let that define your future. Let the mistakes you made at those moments when you lost your temper be lessons to learn from, which make you work to improve your temper. Weaknesses are not death sentences, nor are past mistakes arising from weaknesses confirmation that you cannot change. Beating up on yourself for past mistakes is the only thing that can keep you hanging on to the past. Learn to let the past be in the past and focus on how to improve the present.

- **Decrease negative self-chatter.** Your emotional state of mind actually determines your thoughts about what is happening in and around you. Your emotional state of mind is affected by your self-talk. In order to improve your emotional intelligence level, you need to watch the inner conversations you hold with yourself. If the content of your inner chatter is leaning towards being dominantly negative, you are more likely to think irrationally about the situation happening in or around you. That means you are more likely to react to impulses from a negative state of mind.

- **Improve your concentration level.** Your EQ level is affected by how well you can manage your attention span. We live in a world that is full of constant distractions from text messages, emails, social media, TV, and so on. How long can you keep your focus in the face of all these distractions? Remember that your daily productivity level is directly tied to how focused you are on the tasks that you take on. If you cannot listen actively to your child, colleague, or spouse without taking a look at your phone, where does that leave you on the emotional intelligence scale? This is a very important aspect to take into consideration as you work on improving yourself in a world where the act of socializing has become increasingly distracting.

- **Read non-verbal clues.** To improve your connection with others, you need to hone your non-verbal reading skills. Look beyond what their words are saying to what their gestures, body movements, and facial expressions are conveying. These clues are a huge giveaway of people's emotions – you can decipher them and sense a whole lot of what they are meaning besides what they are saying.

EQ Tests Versus Personality Assessment

Is there really a difference between personality assessment and EQ assessment? If someone takes a personality test before they are hired in an organization, for example, is that not a form of EQ assessment? The answer to that is an emphatic no!

Personality tests, which, by the way, form the basis for many organizations' psychometric tests, are a great tool to learn about the individuals in an organization or team. Nevertheless, there are some drawbacks to personality testing which makes it necessary to not depend *only* on them if growth is truly desired by organizations or individuals.

One of the major drawbacks of personality tests is that they do not identify the development or improvement needs of the individual. By its very definition, personality is the essence of a person's character. It is said to be stable throughout a person's lifetime since it is encoded into a person's genetic makeup. What this means is that your personality can be fairly predictable. You can bump into an old friend and still tell how they will behave under certain conditions because of the type of personality they have.

This is both good news and bad news. It is good news because you can say with a certain level of accuracy what your traits, as well as other people's traits, are. Organizations can use that information to know who fits what job. Friends and family, as well as team members, can determine who is a good fit for a particular task.

However, the bad news is that a personality test keeps you in a tight box. It gives you a label that is fixed for life but doesn't in any way point to what needs to be improved. It is like a life sentence. *"You are an extroverted and dominant personality type,*" period! There is no suggestion as to what areas of your personality can be used to your benefit and what areas are to be worked upon.

At best, personality tests offer a deep understanding of the inherent character of the test-taker, but they don't go further to provide remedies for their emotional flaws.

Bottom Line

Whatever your EQ test score is, you should continue to work on it with a goal of improving it. If your EQ test score is below average, there is no need to lose hope, as improvement is always possible. This book has offered several tips and tools that you can use to begin to work on yourself and eventually improve your emotional intelligence. If your EQ test score is on the high side, I congratulate you. However, keep in mind that you need to show empathy towards those who have low EQ scores. Equally, realize that a person who has high emotional intelligence tends to neglect their own needs in a bid to "be there" for others. People will look up to you for advice and guidance; create time for them, but don't neglect yourself also.

Chapter 9: Emotional Intelligence: The Dark Side

Emotional intelligence is a powerful tool. A person who has masterful control of his or her responses can become a very powerful leader, influencer, or team player. In as much as these factors can be considered as great positive qualities, they can also be used to influence others negatively. A powerful team player can either foster positive team spirit among team members, or subtly influence the team to play his or her game. A man or woman can either influence his or her spouse to aspire to their best selves or influence the spouse to become subjected to their control. Parents can be authoritative yet be a positive influence on their children, or, be strict and assert control over the behaviors of their children.

One leader stood on the podium long ago and spoke words that echoed throughout history, *"I have a dream!"* There was every reason for him to negatively influence his people into violence but, in spite of the emotions bursting inside of him, he channeled his speech and actions towards well-thought-out behaviors. The outcome: Dr. Martin Luther King, Jr. became famous as one of the greatest black American activists of all time.

One other leader who also stood on the podium long ago and screamed at the top of his lungs influenced his people to the point that it became mind control. Adolf Hitler literally marched his people into mindless war. The result: The Second World War and the Holocaust, both events which claimed the lives of over 40 million people.

One way or the other, a powerful influencing tool was utilized to affect the behavior of others.

Positive Influence versus Control

It is easy to mistake influence for control. In the wrong hands, emotional intelligence can become a dangerous controlling tool. Instead of positively influencing the behavior of others, it can be used to control others to behave the way the influencer deems right.

But then it can be argued that positive influence is also a form of control. For example, if a person chooses to be rude and say nasty things about you in the workplace but then you assert your EQ and calmly responded intelligently to their nasty comments, you have successfully controlled your behavior in response to theirs. In addition, you may have influenced them to start thinking about their own behavior – how stupidly they have behaved. You may not have directly told them they acted unwisely, but your behavior did say it loud and clear. Now, they feel ashamed of their behavior and may even want to adjust to acting more like you in the future. Somehow, you are controlling their thinking process without as much as lifting a finger.

However, there's a difference – a huge difference, between positive influence and control. To influence others positively is **to shift their focus to the best they can be**. To control others is **to restrict their focus to how you want them to be**. One leads to freedom; the other leads to bondage. Dr. King led people to freedom; Hitler led people to bondage. Nelson Mandela, South Africa's first indigenous president, led people to freedom through positive influence. Joseph Stalin, dictator of the USSR (1929 to 1953) led people to bondage and death through control.

Protecting Yourself from Emotional Saboteurs

But this chapter is not about world leaders. It is about you and how you can protect yourself from negative influence or control. It is about showing you how to keep your emotions from being fired up by people who may want to take advantage of you to promote their own personal agenda. It is about making sure that you continuously keep your EQ at the highest possible level you can in order to protect yourself from outbursts that are influenced by external deliberate mind control.

You do not necessarily have to be under someone's authority before they can negatively influence you. It doesn't matter whether or not you are a subordinate, subject, follower, student, child, sibling, or any other person who is under some sort of authority; these are not the only persons who can be negatively influenced. A person under another's authority can also control the person in authority if they know how to manipulate emotions. If you have heard or seen a child holding its parents to ransom, or a boss not being able to fully exercise their authority over a particular subordinate, then you have witnessed a form of an emotional saboteur.

Simply put, when someone hijacks your ability to think and act rationally, no matter how briefly, they are exerting their control over your emotions and are capable of making you do what they want. If you do not know how to keep yourself protected against such shrewd and devious influencers, they can run your life aground no matter how intelligent you are in other aspects of life.

Emotional control can be present in your professional or personal relationships, and that control can make you feel incapacitated to do or say exactly what it is you wish to do or say. Perhaps one of the main reasons for this is fear. There is a fear of:

1. **Loss of opportunity**: being docile so as to gain or keep an opportunity such as employment or other benefits.

2. **Confrontation**: wanting to avoid conflicts or arguments that may arise from taking your stand against emotional control.

3. **Loss of partnership or friendship**: trying to keep a relationship by all means even if that means subjecting yourself to negative influence.

4. **Loss of basic needs**: if you are in a relationship that makes you completely dependent on the other partner for your basic needs of survival, you tend to do as they wish so as not to lose your only means of daily sustenance.

5. **Discomfort**: avoiding the feeling of uneasiness and awkwardness that is sure to arise if you refuse to yield control.

If you have any of these fears, it is a clear sign that you are in a relationship that is most likely controlling you. Keep in mind also that control may not always show up as someone trying to dominate you. It can come in ways that appear to be very pleasing at first, like subtly 'bribing' you into doing something and then later turning it into emotional blackmail. In other words, *"you'll get this if you do that"* becomes *"you'll not get this unless you do that!"* But no matter how emotional and psychological control manifest at first, in the long run, it doesn't feel good. It robs you of your innate ability and desire to explore your world, and subjects you to a world of negative self-image, negative self-talk, and shame.

So, how do you identify behaviors from other people that indicate that they are controlling or trying to control you, and how do you set yourself free from such emotional control? In other words, how do you sharpen your emotional intelligence to keep you guarded against emotional saboteurs? Here are some of the most prominent behaviors you will notice from others who are trying to negatively influence or control you, and what you can do about it.

Playing the victim / weak party

This is one of the oldest tricks in the book. Even children use it to gain emotional control over their parents and other adults. When someone who is clearly not weak or incapable of doing a thing, suddenly begins to behave as if they are being forced to do something that they are incapable of, they are playing with your emotions. They are appearing weak so that they can take advantage of your soft side and get you to cut corners, do the wrong thing, or bend the rules for their sake. For example, a lady may pretend to be too fragile to handle a task so that her male boss will assign her a simpler task. She's trying to capitalize on the soft spot many men naturally have for women. This is emotional blackmail.

Keep your emotions protected from such blackmail by first understanding the capacity of the other person. Are they truly incapable or are they simply pretending? Secondly, do not have double standards if you are in charge of people whether at work, school, or at home. Do not lower your standards to suit one person because if you do, others will also capitalize on it or, the same person will want to continue to receive that preferential treatment.

Too many expectations, rules, and demands

If you are in a relationship that is demanding too much from you, it is a clear sign that someone is controlling you. Whether it is a professional or personal relationship, too many demands and expectations from you can cripple your ability to think and act rationally. With time, all your emotions about that relationship will begin to become negative because of the pressure on you. Gradually, the rules, demands, and expectations will have sapped out everything that could bring you joy and happiness in that relationship. In extreme cases, the mere thought of that relationship can cause your emotions to go all out of whack, and you to behave accordingly. In a professional relationship like a job, you will begin to hate the job and effectively deprive yourself of putting in your best or being more productive. Your focus will gradually shift from performing at your peak to seeking better alternatives – a better job.

In a personal relationship such as that of a couple, parent-child relationship, or in a friendship, the strain caused by all the demands and expectations can trigger resentment towards the other person. Eventually, your focus will no longer be on how to enjoy more of the other person's company, but will be on how to either fight off your build-up of resentment, or how to show them that you are uncomfortable with their behavior.

If you feel such control in a professional relationship, one way to protect yourself from such emotional sabotage is to first recognize what the other person (superior or colleague) is doing. They may not even be intentionally targeting you in particular. It could be their general behavior. If that is the case, you would do well to understand why they behave that way – what drives them underneath, that is not showing on the surface. If you can understand them, you can definitely change your reaction towards them. If they are targeting you in particular, then you should not respond in anger or by being annoyed because doing so will show them that they have you in their grip. Simply cut down contact with them as much as is permissible in the professional environment. When you have significantly mastered your responses, speak to them about their attitude without being argumentative or appearing confrontational.

Keeping guard of your emotions in a personal relationship that is threatened by this type of control means that you must talk to the other person about their controlling habit without being angry yourself. Another thing to keep in mind is that you must stop yourself from thinking that *you* are responsible for making them happy by living up to *their* expectations and demands. As far as you can, do what you can do but do not displease yourself just to make someone else happy. If you must please them, think long and hard about the effects such an action will have on your emotional stability.

Sudden positive change in attitude towards you

When someone who you've known to be unfriendly towards you or who generally doesn't like you much all of a sudden begins to warm their way to you, you need to be careful. It is true that people change, but when someone goes from mean to nice and very suddenly does so, it could be that they are trying to be nice to you because they want to take advantage of you.

To keep yourself from falling prey to such tactics, you need to be wary of how much you let them into your personal life. Take their sudden niceness with a pinch of salt and don't trust them completely. Think very hard before sharing information with them, especially if it is of a personal or private nature. They may be looking for a way to blackmail you emotionally.

Making you feel less than them

One characteristic of a controlling person is their constant need to be acknowledged as being better than the other person. They may subtly imply that you ought to be grateful you have them, and that you should continue to please them in order to keep them around because obviously, you are less than them. They rub their accomplishments in your face or make you feel less attractive than they are. Their aim is to subdue and dominate you.

In order to protect yourself from such humiliating relationships, do not ever cower to their demands. Recognize that you are perfectly okay the way you are and if they are not satisfied with you, you should begin to consider if staying in the relationship is worth the constant humiliation. Remember that for another person to successfully control you, they must have some sort of upper hand. Do not give them the upper hand in your relationship. Make them see that even though you are not in competition with them, you play an equally important role in the relationship.

Extreme monitoring

This may show up in several ways, but first, let me be clear about what I mean by extreme monitoring. When a loved one calls you because they are worried about your whereabouts or because they care, that should be expected. When your boss checks in once in a while to learn about your progress with a current project, it is normal and should be expected. However, when calls and check-ins gravitate from care and concern to undue micromanaging, then the other person may be trying to control you in some way. Extreme monitoring can show up in any of the following examples:

- When a spouse begins to monitor and control where their partner should be and go, how long they should be out of their sight, and exactly what they should or shouldn't be doing, that is an extreme case of monitoring that shouldn't be taken lightly. They may even go to the extent of snooping, spying, or demanding continuous disclosure.

  Talk to the controlling partner about their behavior with a calm attitude. Don't come across as being confrontational or angry, as that can likely spark up a heated exchange. Be honest about how very suffocating and constricting their behavior makes you feel. If they are unwilling to take steps towards correcting such behavior, you should seriously consider if staying in that relationship is really worth the pain.

- When a boss or superior micromanages you out of his or her sheer need to be in control, or out of their own fears and insecurities, then you have someone who may be sabotaging your emotions without even realizing it.

Your best bet for protecting yourself from this type of emotional sabotage is by clearly letting the person with the controlling attitude know that you don't like being micromanaged. If telling them directly is not appropriate, ensure that they get the message loud and clear by staying on top of your responsibilities so that there will be no point checking in on you so often. You can also use your initiative and be more productive beyond your job description (within reason) to prove to them that you need little to no supervision.

- When someone goes out of their way to keep tabs on you either online or offline to see whether or not you are making progress, you may have someone who is stalking you for the purpose of manipulating you.

  Keep personal information away from these types of people as much as possible. Do not give complete trust to someone who wants to connect with you by any means necessary. Their desperation is a dead giveaway that they may not have the purest of intentions.

- When someone delegates power to you or lends you something but is constantly on your neck to see how you are using the power or what they gave you. They are either out there letting everyone know that you are a beneficiary of their benevolence, or they are choking and suffocating you to death by making sure you are not 'overstepping' your boundary. It may also be that they are constantly keeping score of everything they help you with.

It is likely that there is an underlying issue of trust and lack of respect for your feelings in this case. But before you begin to express your honest feelings to them, give thought to whether doing so will actually change anything. It is possible that they are in a chronic habit that cannot be changed easily. If that is the case, simply avoid seeking their help and taking up their offers. In the case where you think they may be willing to change, make them understand that you are not comfortable with their monitoring behaviors.

Making you feel guilty using staunch moral/religious standards

One form of control which may not be apparent to many is the use of moral or religious standards to make others feel guilty. When you find yourself faced with choosing between following someone else's prescribed moral/religious standards and following your heart, it is very likely that you are being backed into a corner that will leave you feeling guilty or dissatisfied. Guilty if you follow your heart, and, dissatisfied if you follow their standards. When someone places you in this type of situation, they are practically draining you of your power think rationally because they are pitching you against an authority (usually, God) whom you feel compelled to obey even when deep down in your heart, you know it doesn't suit you to conform to their standards.

Do not grant anybody the permission to play over your emotional intelligence by cajoling you to do something you don't want to, regardless of whether or not they *"come in the name of the Lord."* Hold on to your personal convictions about your beliefs and if you find yourself feeling guilty about something you have said or done, simply own it – make it right, and go about with your life in the most guiltless manner that you can!

Acting in dishonest ways

Sometimes you have that gut feeling that someone is being dishonest even when their actions are showing that they like you, or they are being nice to you. Disregarding the telltale signs of dishonest behaviors may lead you to trust someone you shouldn't.

When something just doesn't seem right no matter how good and dandy their outward appearance seems to be, then you should consider listening to your gut. Be sure you are not misjudging the other person by asking yourself the following questions and providing honest answers:

- Am I jealous, envious, or just angry at the other person?

- Am I holding a grudge due to some past hurt or wrongdoing?

- Am I judging them based on what others have told me about them, or from my own personal encounters with them?

- Do I have trust issues?

If you are honest and sincere with yourself, you will know if you are feeling bad vibes about that person because of a preconceived notion, or purely because of your natural instincts.

Keeping you away from friends and family

When someone is systematically isolating you from the people that are closest to you so that they can have you all to themselves, it is a very strong indication that they are trying to control you. It may begin with complaints about how long you hang out with family and friends, and then gradually shift to complaints about particular individuals like *"I don't like your sister"* or *"Why do you spend more time with your friend than you do with me?"* These complaints may initially sound genuine but with time, they can grow into serious threats. You might be asked to choose between them and your friends/family. The game plan here is simple: strip you of every support system you can rely on so that you have only them to turn to. That way, you are at their mercy.

If you are in this type of relationship, you have to seek help as fast as you can, really. Take time to evaluate your chances of safety if you should confront them. If your chances of safety are slim, seek external help. Reconnect with your support system and get out of that relationship.

Bottom Line

The need to continuously improve EQ is not the exclusive prerogative of powerful world leaders or business executives. Everyday life requires that you call on your EQ when the need arises. Being vigilant of our interactions with others and asking ourselves every now and then if we are being influenced negatively is a key to keeping behaviors in check. Being emotionally intelligent is not just about being nice; it is also about being proactive and keeping yourself safe.

Finally, remember that your overall well-being is directly linked to your emotional state of being. Do all you can to keep that part of you as healthy as possible. *"When our emotional health is in a bad state, so is our level of self-esteem. We have to slow down and deal with what is troubling us, so that we can enjoy the simple joy of being happy and at peace with ourselves"* (Scott, 2012).

Conclusion

Thanks again for taking the time to read this book!

You should now have a good understanding of emotional intelligence, how it is tested, and how to improve upon it. Now is the time to put the information in this book into practice and begin improving upon your own EQ!

References

Ackerman, C. (2018). What is emotional intelligence? + 18 ways to improve it. https://positivepsychologyprogram.com/emotional-intelligence-eq/

Begiri, G. (2018). The 5 features of emotional intelligence. https://virtualspeech.com/blog/5-features-emotional-intelligence

Bonior, A. (2015). 20 Signs Your Partner Is Controlling. https://www.psychologytoday.com/intl/blog/friendship-20/201506/20-signs-your-partner-is-controlling

Bradberry, T. (2019). 9 signs you're dealing with an emotional manipulator. https://www.theladders.com/career-advice/9-signs-youre-dealing-with-an-emotional-manipulator

Career Builder (2011). Seventy-one percent of employers say they value emotional intelligence over IQ, according to career builder survey. https://www.careerbuilder.ca/share/aboutus/pressreleasesdetail.aspx?id=pr652&sd=8%2f18%2f2011&ed=8%2f18%2f2099

Cherry, K. (2019). IQ vs. EQ: Which one is more important? https://www.verywellmind.com/iq-or-eq-which-one-is-more-important-2795287

Duggal, N. (2019). Emotional intelligence in the workplace: Why you need it, how to get it. https://www.simplilearn.com/emotional-intelligence-what-why-and-how-article

Freedman, J. (2010). The six seconds EQ model. https://www.6seconds.org/2010/01/27/the-six-seconds-eq-model/

Fairbank, R. (2017). The blood-brain barrier: Controlling behaviors. http://www.uh.edu/nsm/feature/graduate-students/controlling-behavior/.

Hill, T. (2018). 9 signs you are being emotionally controlled & how to stop it.
https://blogs.psychcentral.com/caregivers/2017/09/5385/

James, S. (2018). Know thyself: Why self-awareness is the greatest gift you can give yourself.
https://medium.com/@stefanjames/know-thyself-why-self-awareness-is-the-greatest-gift-you-can-give-yourself-2c6d5e33d2ef

McGill University (2014). New evidence confirms link between IQ, brain cortex.
https://www.sciencedaily.com/releases/2014/03/140304141734.htm

Petor, J. (2017). Why measuring emotional intelligence is important. https://blog.psionline.com/talent/why-measuring-emotional-intelligence-is-important

Reddy, C. (2016). Emotional intelligence: How to measure and assess. https://content.wisestep.com/emotional-intelligence-measure-assess/

Thomas, I. S., (2012). Intentional Dissonance. Central Avenue Publishing.

Scott, J. C. (2012). Clear: A guide to treating acne naturally. CreateSpace Independent Publishing Platform.

www.ingramcontent.com/pod-product-compliance
Lightning Source LLC
LaVergne TN
LVHW011724060526
838200LV00051B/3010